Consider The Lilies:
A Personal Story of Healing, Health, and Heaven

Consider The Lilies:

A Personal Story of Healing, Health, and Heaven

Millard C. Reed

Trevecca Press
Nashville • Tennessee • 1998

ISBN 0-9657278-2-3

Printed in the United States of America.
2 3 4 5 • 99 98

Cover design by David Malone of Malone Creative.

Cover art used by permission of the artist—
Sharon Hults of Hults Art and Design, Boulder, CO.

Permission to quote from the following copyrighted versions of the Bible is acknowledged with appreciation:

All Scripture quotations not otherwise designated are from *The New English Bible*® (NEB®). Copyright © 1970 by Cambridge University Press. All rights reserved.

The Message. Copyright © 1993. Used by permission of NavPress Publishing Group. All rights reserved.

The *New King James* (NKJ). Copyright © 1982 Thomas Nelson, Inc. Used by permission. All rights reserved.

Scripture quotations marked (NIV) are taken from the *Holy Bible, New International Version*®. NIV®. Copyright © 1963, 1978, 1984 by International Bible Society. Used by permission of Zondervan Publishing House. All rights reserved.

The *Williams New Testament, The New Testament in the Language of the People,* by Charles B. Williams. Copyright © 1937, 1966, 1986 by Holman Bible Publishers. Used by permission.

Lyrics from "I Sing Praises" by Terry MacAlmon (Copyright © 1989 by Intregrity's Hosanna! Music/ASCAP) are used by permission from the publisher.

Dedication

To all who prayed for me,
especially my family,
and more particularly my dear wife, Barbara

Acknowledgments

I am grateful for the contributions of these persons: Neil Wiseman, who persuaded me that folks would want to hear the story; Delores Green, who created the first draft from my word processor efforts; Jan Greathouse, who served as my benevolent editor; and Marian Jewell, who scrutinized the details.

Contents

Introduction

I have a story to tell you. It is not my story, however. It is God's story, one in which I had a part. God's stories are always "rescue" stories. He is the One who rescued the very universe by bringing order out of chaos in the creation.

He "rescued" Abram from Ur of the Chaldees to make of him the "Father of the Faithful."

He "rescued" Israel out of Egypt to make a "people" of those who were "no people."

He "rescued" Jesus from the confines of the tomb to declare Him the Lord of Glory.

And He promises to rescue the Church when He comes in the air to take away His "bride."

These are the major plot lines in God's great rescue story.

But there are many, many minor subplots that are also rescue stories. Each of them is a complement to the larger story. Each of us has a role in the grand divine drama. You do and I do. The one that I tell in this book is not different in kind—only in detail.

As I share this story of a miraculous healing, please hear it as my modest report on the role that I found myself playing in God's drama for His glory. Mine was not a "lead role"; I was unconscious during many of the key events. There is no sense in which my prayer or my faith brought about my healing. I am not the "rescuer"; I am the "rescued."

And none of the hundreds who shared this healing drama with me, including family, physicians, and friends, would be inclined to take any credit for causing the healing to take place. You will find no "how-to-be-healed formula" here. What you will find is an authentic account of God's physical rescue in one instance. It is an account that will affirm your confidence in the sovereign and benevolent nature of our Father's plans for all of us.

Here are the simple facts of my situation. (1) My liver "died" because of hepatitis gone fulminant. (2) The only hope given for survival was a transplant, and (3) the surgery, it was judged, needed to take place within ten days. (4) Then, without medical provocation, a new liver generated spontaneously.

It is the intent of this brief book to provide the further details in such a way that God will be glorified and that many will come to an awareness of who God is and who they are in Him.

This obvious activity of God in my life has brought me new insights which I share at the end of each section. I pray they will help you.

Millard C. Reed

Chapter 1
New Life in Nashville

He rescued us from the domain of darkness and brought us away into the kingdom of his dear Son, in whom our release is secured and our sins forgiven.

Colossians 1:13 (NEB)

God rescued us from dead-end alleys and dark dungeons. He's set us up in the kingdom of the Son he loves so much, the Son who got us out of the pit we were in, got rid of the sins we were doomed to keep repeating.

Colossians 1:13 (*The Message*)

I could hear the sounds of a voice, but though I tried with all my might, I could discern no language—just sounds as one might hear in a foreign country or as an infant might hear when he or she catches a parent's emotion but has not yet learned the language.

Actually, the voice seemed to be very much like that of a parent: soft, patient, and kind. It made me really want to understand. I concentrated even more earnestly to make sense of the sounds, but without success. I was thankful the voice did not stop. It spoke again and again as if I could hear and comprehend. It was so appealing, so inviting that I yearned to understand and respond.

My rescue story does not begin with a review of my qualifications. My story begins with my lostness.

Then, little by little, in scattered phrases at first, I began to hear questions— simple, childlike questions.

"Do you know where you are?"

That phrase was the first one that made sense to me, but I had no idea how to answer. Some nonverbal response emerged as a raspy sound from my throat. It did not sound like me. But the voice seemed encouraged by my feeble sound.

"Do you know where you have been?"

My silence seemed to be understood by the voice as a no.

"Do you know what day this is?"

My first clear word was "no." The fact that I was actually communicating with a person, although in the most childlike way, filled me with emotion. I sensed myself beginning to weep.

"That is all right!" the voice affirmed me. Then it continued, "Do you know who I am?"

"No, I don't. I am sorry!" I said as I continued to weep quietly.

"Do you know what you do?"

At this question, I concentrated hard. Surely, I should know this. I remembered that what I did had been very important to me. But I had no inkling, not even one, of what it was. The voice was patient. "No," I finally said.

"Can you tell me your name?" The voice waited. "Can you tell me who you are? Can you tell me your name?"

My earlier joy in being able to communicate with the pleasant voice was fading. Fear, mingled with despair, washed over me. I could not answer any question that I was asked. I could not say where I had been, where I was, or what I do. Try as hard as I would, I could not identify myself. I was truly and completely and—it seemed to me at the moment—hopelessly lost. I could find no point of reference. There was no "guiding star" in this dark night, no "true north" on my compass.

Soon the voice began to take on the qualities of a person. A man was at my side, holding my hand in both of his. They were warm and reassuring. "That is all right!" he said and patted my hand as if to leave me.

"No, please don't leave me!" I said, with a voice that still did not sound like mine. "Let's go over those questions again, and this time you give me the right answers."

"Of course, I will," said the doctor, and there followed the most treasured brief conversation of my new life. "My name is Dr. Burk. I am your physician. You have been, and still are, very ill. You became ill while preaching in South Carolina."

"That's it," I thought to myself. "That's what I do! I preach the Gospel of my Savior Jesus Christ." It was so wonderful to rediscover that part of my identity. South Carolina? I could not remember.

The doctor went on. "You are now leading Trevecca Nazarene College."

"Could that be?" my mind questioned. "Has that happened? When did I become a college president? I remember Trevecca, but am I a part of it?"

Then, with a concluding squeeze of my hand he said, "And your name is Millard Reed."

That's right! My heart seemed to skip a beat within me. That is my name! That is who I am! I am not "nobody." I am somebody. I am Millard!

Even in that half-conscious state, I was amused at myself. That name, which my parents had given me in honor of the man who had been preaching when my father was converted, had always troubled me. From my childhood, I dreaded the first day of school because as often as not the teacher would mispronounce it, "Mildred Reed." All the children who had known me from the previous year would laugh, and I would be so embarrassed. While in high school, I was the quarterback on the football team, but I would routinely get a few votes for football queen. Some few "buddies" of mine would put my name on the ballot and then think it great fun to hear the report, "And three votes for Mildred Reed." I respect the name, but I have always enjoyed being called "Pastor Reed." There is no confusion of gender.

As much as I had been embarrassed by the name throughout my lifetime, IT SOUNDED ABSOLUTELY BEAUTIFUL when Dr. Burk said it. I thought to myself, "How wonderful to know who the doctor is, to know what I do, and where I do it. And most of all, it is wonderful to know who I am!"

You will notice that my return to consciousness began by Dr. Burk's telling me who he was. With his having established that authority, I could then come to believe who I was—really, who I had been all the while but did not realize.

In a similar manner, the voice of God breaks into our spiritual lostness in order to make himself known to us. And as we turn to Him and accept His authority, He lets us know not only who He is but also who we are as His beloved.

The brief conversation with my doctor on the first Sunday of March 1996, after nearly eight days of unconsciousness, is in the middle of my healing story. But it is also the beginning point. In the following brief chapters the other details will fall into place. But remember the point of beginning: my total lostness to which God responds with a "rescue" which is an expression of His sovereign and benevolent nature. I cannot truly know who I am or my mission in life until I know who God is and what are His patterns for me.

Discoveries on the Way

My rescue story does not begin with a review of my qualifications as Christian, pastor, or college president. My story begins with my lostness.

My crucial moment of return came as I had the simple sense to ask for help from one who, I sensed, knew more than I did. He provided orientation when I was totally disoriented.

I will continue to be open to God's word of orientation.

Chapter 2
Another Way of Showing Off

So, then, if with Christ you've put all that pretentious and infantile religion behind you, why do you let yourselves be bullied by it? "Don't touch this! Don't taste that! Don't go near this!" Do you think things that are here today and gone tomorrow are worth that kind of attention? Such things sound impressive if said in a deep enough voice. They even give the illusion of being pious and humble and ascetic. But they're just another way of showing off, making you look important.
Colossians 2:21-23 *(The Message)*

Like most of us who were reared in the Church, I have had a high regard for the stewardship of the body. The holiness tradition, of which I am an enthusiastic part, has always spoken out against anything that would do us physical harm.

And we do not view discipline as a simple matter of personal taste but as a matter of keeping "the temple of the Holy Spirit" sacred. Beverage alcohol, tobacco, and other drugs are strictly prohibited. Some people of my tradition might concede that one who "drinks" or "smokes" could possibly make it to heaven, but that one would surely be a "special case." I remember one of our old-timers saying, "A man who chews tobacco might go to heaven, but where would he go to spit?"

> *I tell my story to help you who, like me, are so committed to the service of the Lord that you underestimate your own fatigue and even your own sickness.*

My own family was especially conservative. As a matter of "personal conviction," my dad felt he could not drink coffee. He had been delivered from tobacco at the time of his conversion. Sometime later, he had not been able to get his morning coffee and found himself with a headache and irritable. He felt he heard the Holy Spirit ask of him, "How is your coffee addiction different from tobacco?" That was the end of coffee for him. We served coffee to our guests, but it was not a part of the family routine.

While my rearing had these "negatives," the far greater emphasis was upon the positive aspects of physical stewardship. I am not sure that my preacher dad had this all worked out theologically. He just felt, deep down, that hard work was good for a person. He was saved and called to preach out of a large farm family—a family in which hard work was almost a competitive sport, with each one quietly, and sometimes not so quietly, trying to outdo the other.

Dad's brothers never quite seemed to understand that a preacher really does work hard. They couldn't imagine one's working while wearing a white shirt and a tie. Or, at least, they acted as if they did not understand. I think their hint that a preacher is lazy always bothered Dad. I know that he worked hard at the job because he loved the Lord and wanted to please his Heavenly Father. But I also think he did not want his earthly brothers to think he was lazy. His passion for hard work may have been part of the reason why he died too soon at the age of fifty-eight.

He also felt, as I do, that one of the basic things a dad can do for a boy is teach him how to work. I was the fourth son to become "unofficial janitor" at the church. And when there were workdays at the church, we boys were always there to work a little harder than the next one.

Couple this background with a fanatical, old football coach by the name of Winn (that was really his name) who kept barking with staccato emphasis, "When the going gets tough, the tough get going." You can begin to understand my mindset. When my friend, a physiologist, pointed out that I could improve my health by faithful exercise and careful diet, I committed to the discipline. During more than twenty years, I have jogged for a total of some eight thousand miles. I have logged nearly six thousand miles in my beloved, nearby Shelby Park.

Several years ago, I collaborated with C. S. Cowles to write a book on the values of "temple conditioning." It was widely used as a study guide for Sunday school classes discussing the subject.

I hope I have impressed you by now. I HAVE LIVED A DISCIPLINED LIFE! Since the first Sunday of March, however, I am done with "showing off." I ask you who are like me to watch the unfolding of my story and see if there is anything familiar to you about it. (Better yet, ask your spouse if it seems familiar!) Maybe you can be wiser than I was.

It is true that physical conditioning has had its reward. Discipline and the goodness of God made it possible for me to have an unblemished attendance record in thirty-five years of pastoral work and five years with the College. I never had to miss a service for ill health. Not one. Fifteen of those pastoral years I preached twice each Sunday morning and once each evening. *Never* an absence!

Do you hear pride in that last comment? I think it is there. Maybe even arrogance. It pleased me to hear "Pastor Reed is ALWAYS there when you need him." And sometimes the desire to hear that statement drove me beyond what reasonable stewardship of the mind and body ought to have called for.

Please consider my mindset as I begin to fill in the details of my trip to Charleston, South Carolina, the deadly illness, and the miraculous healing.

Pastor Charles Fountain of the St. Andrews Church of the Nazarene in Charleston had scheduled me a year or so in advance to be with his congregation. We had gone over the details for a weekend of services, and I was eager to be with him and his people. I was scheduled to fly out of Nashville on Friday midday, arrive in time for the Friday night service, and then preach Saturday night, as well as Sunday morning and Sunday afternoon. A full schedule? Not quite. Since there were donors to the college in the area, I would also have a luncheon meeting and a dinner meeting on Saturday. (Does such a tight schedule sound familiar to anyone?)

With such "important meetings" on the agenda, a fellow like me (and some of you) tends to ignore a small matter like a growing physical discomfort. Right?! To be fair to myself, I must point out that it was a discomfort that I could not describe. Not a pain really. Just a sense that something was not quite right. By Tuesday, preceding my trip, I was surprised to sense that I simply could not eat. I did not have a lack of appetite. I literally could not eat.

While sharing with a group of faculty at Trevecca on Thursday, I mentioned my general discomfort to our staff doctor, Mike Moredock. He is a little embarrassed to acknowledge it now, but he said what was reasonable at that time and under those circumstances: "You probably have the old-fashioned flu. Take a couple of Tylenols."

I did what I would always do at such times. I went to Shelby Park and jogged an extra long time—about an hour. I was going to work it out. "When the going gets tough, the tough get going"—remember?

Then I went home to do what Dr. Moredock had suggested—take two Tylenols and go to bed. About midnight, I awoke in a drenching sweat. I mean, water could be wrung from my pajamas. My pillow, not just the pillowcase, was soaked. I woke my wife, Barbara, to show her what had happened to me. But I concluded that the fever had broken and that I would be all right to leave the next morning for Charleston. (Does this sound like anyone you know?)

The next morning Barbara begged me not to go. What do you think I did? That's right! I insisted that "I am a bit better" and "the people are expecting me." I did think, "If I see Dr. Mike on campus I will tell him about the sweating." But I did not happen to see him, so I boarded the plane for South Carolina. I had made it to the pulpit on other occasions when I didn't feel too well, and the Lord had blessed. Surely He would again this time.

When Pastor Fountain met me at the airport in Charleston, he routinely asked me how I was. I was truthful and told him that I did not feel well but was sure that I would soon be better. I deferred when he offered a nice evening meal, choosing to lie down for a while. I was buoyed by preaching in the evening service but noticed that I had little energy to chat with the people following the service.

I slept well Friday night but found myself feeling worse rather than better the next morning. A Saturday luncheon was to have been arranged upon my arrival. I did not follow through—my first concession to not feeling well. But the dinner meeting was to be very special. The pastor and his wife, good friends Dr. and Mrs. Rashford, Dr. and Mrs. Hazell (he had lectured the previous year at Trevecca), and Mr. and Mrs. Bob Pelham (a former Board member and dear friend to the College) were to meet me at our favorite seafood place, The Crab House on James Island. We had met there a couple of years earlier. Seafood is a favorite for me, and this restaurant is one of the best places anywhere.

But, in spite of all this wonderful atmosphere and these wonderful friends, I could not eat. While others ordered meals that I would have loved to enjoy, I finally ordered a cup of clam chowder and tried to talk about the progress of the school while others enjoyed their meals.

We went directly from the restaurant to the church. For the first time, I wondered if I would be able to preach. While the people gathered, I meditated and prayed, seated on the first pew. The Lord helped me and the people were kind. Brother Bob Pelham later wrote me a note and said, "I could tell you were not feeling well. You acted as though you had the flu—[and looked] pale and tired. You preached beautifully but said you felt as though you were not keeping your sermon organized. Everyone could see you were speaking from your heart as God was leading you."

Following the service, the pastor and his wife, thinking I might feel more like eating then, invited me to go with them to a restaurant. Shoney's soup was no better than The Crab House's had been. Louise Fountain, who is a nurse, suggested that I try Tylenol again. I took two tablets before going to bed.

I awoke suddenly about midnight with awful sweats. (Nothing against Tylenol, but I have resolved NEVER to take one again.) The rest of the night I chilled and began a series of dry heaves until morning. I recount these details neither to brag nor to complain but to illustrate to what lengths many of us will go to "tough it out."

I hope the morning message made sense. Pastor Fountain has admitted, as I have quizzed him, that some thoughts did not seem to hang together. But then, again, that characteristic may not always be a sign of illness—or else many of us are often ill.

The weekend was to feature an international luncheon at noon on Sunday. How I wanted just to go lie down. But as the honored guest, I was to lead the line through the wonderful buffet provided by the ladies of the congregation—more than one of whom pointed out her specialty, suggesting that I would certainly enjoy it. I was quite sure that I would not enjoy anything, but I felt I must take some of each.

Across the room, I spotted my special friend, Bob Pelham, and sat with him to eat—more accurately, to go through the pretense of eating. As I sat there, I began to chill and shake noticeably. Bob observed my shaking and asked me what was wrong with me. Within a few minutes he had medical doctors Rashford and Hazell examining me. They insisted that I go immediately to the hospital. Do you think I obeyed? Here is how Bob described my response: "I had lunch with you on Sunday. I knew you were ill and begged you not to preach that afternoon. You would not relent, saying God had called you to Charleston to do a job and you had to do it. You made it through the service."

I waited in the side room of the platform for the time of the afternoon service. Pastor Fountain thoughtfully started the service earlier than scheduled. Dr. Hazell and Dr. Rashford checked me out again and submitted to my insistence that I would preach.

My concluding message from Colossians had to do with the redemptive quality of suffering. It drew on Paul's comment, "It is now my happiness to suffer for you" (1:24). Delivering that profound truth was meaningful for me. The people were responsive.

Immediately following the service, Dr. Rashford, who is a cardiopulmonary specialist, took me in his car to the hospital. Under his care, I was given immediate and thorough attention in the emergency room. I assured everyone who attended to me that I would be okay, that I was confident that I had no high temperature. Does that sound like me? Or you? There I was in the hospital telling them about my condition. As events unfolded, I was proved wrong on both counts. My temperature registered 102.8° and I definitely was not okay.

I share this personal story because it is pertinent to the healing story. But I also tell it to help you who, like me, are so committed to the service of the Lord that you underestimate your own fatigue and even your own sickness.

I believe in the careful stewardship of the body. After my recovery, liver specialists, trying to find a rational explanation for my healing, said things like, "Had you been a drinker, you would be a dead man now" and "Your years of physical conditioning may have saved your life."

But they also said that my overly aggressive immune system might have been the reason that common hepatitis went "fulminant." This word was a new one to me, one that no doctor seemed to be able to define. Their best answer was that my healthy immune system attacked the hepatitis infection in my liver so aggressively that it actually destroyed the liver. My own healthy system attacked an infected portion of my body and destroyed it, leaving me no viable option for survival other than a transplant.

Had I depended only on my careful eating and drinking habits or my years of conditioning for my survival, I would have been wrong, woefully wrong—dead wrong!

This is no "show-off" story.

Discoveries on the Way

God created these bodies of ours in His image, and His Spirit dwells within us; therefore, a careful stewardship of them is important.

But this important task is one at which we will ultimately fail. Frailty of the flesh comes sooner or later, and we must be prepared to exchange these mortal bodies for immortal ones.

I will continue to practice good stewardship of the mortal body and will receive His resurrection power in anticipation of my immortal body.

Chapter 3
Christians and Stalwart Followers of Christ Who Live in Charleston

There is no question here of Greek and Jew, circumcised and uncircumcised, barbarian, Scythian, slave and freeman; but Christ is all, and is in all.

Colossians 3:11 (NEB)

He is, moreover, the head of the body, the church. He is its origin, the first to return from the dead, to be in all things alone supreme. For in him the complete being of God, by God's own choice, came to dwell.

Colossians 1:18-19 (NEB)

The city in which my healing drama began is an exceptional city.

"Charles' Towne," named by the English settlers for their king, was founded in 1670 and soon provided access to the southern portion of "The New World" for a stream of visionaries. John and Charles Wesley, missionaries to the American Indians (1736) and eventual founders of Methodism, were among them.

Harmony in diversity is possible only by the sanctifying grace of the Holy Spirit bestowed on the people.

The city thrived from very early on. Of approximately 2,000 buildings in the historic district today, 73 predate the Revolutionary War, 136 date from the late 1700s, and more than 600 others were built in the early 1800s. Much of the city was built by slave labor. Charleston was an entry point for the great mass of slave immigration, and the old slave market can still be visited today.

Significant moments in American history took place in Charleston. It gave America her first significant victory in the Revolutionary War and sounded the first defiant shots of the Civil

War. In the early 1860s Southern aristocrats watched from their antebellum homes on East Battery Street as the Union forces bombarded the Confederates who occupied Fort Sumter in the bay. Submarine warfare was begun in that bay when the Confederate vessel *Hunley* sank the *USS Housatonic.*

But Charleston would prefer to be known not as a city of war but as "the cradle of Southern gentility." Today many of its residents claim that Charleston is the last bastion of this charming way of life. So many tall church steeples pierce the skyline that Charleston has been called "The Holy City." More than twenty picturesque "squares" dot the historic area. Each has a name and a monument or plaque to commemorate some historic moment. Distinctive decorated buildings surround each. In most seasons of the year there is some vivid color. Azaleas in various hues bloom in the spring, and large, ivory-colored magnolias and red and yellow roses bloom in the early summer. The bright fuchsia of the crepe myrtle and the various colors of the perennials exhibit through the summer and fall. And the white camellias bloom through the winter. In most instances, huge live oak trees, decorated by nature with hanging Spanish moss, cast a welcomed shadow over the entire square. The beauty unanimously strikes visitors. And residents are inclined to think their city is without equal. A popular story in Charleston tells of a wealthy matron who, when asked why she didn't travel, responded, "Why should I travel when I am already here?"

As I was welcomed to "Charles' Towne" by my twentieth-century "Charles" (Pastor Charles Fountain), I knew immediately that he had prepared a welcome befitting the city. He asked if I wished to enjoy dinner before or after the evening service. When I decided to wait until after the service, he took me to my quarters at the Middleton Gardens Inn. It had been part of an old rice plantation that had been converted to serve guests. The inn boasted of the "oldest landscaped gardens in America," begun in 1741. One hundred slaves took ten years to complete the terraces. True to their billing, the camellias were already in full bloom. Wild geese and ducks glided across the old rice fields, now clear-as-glass ponds surrounded by white pines with their deep green needles and textured bark. The aroma of pine and camellias was sweet in the air. An old stable yard had been refurbished. It was a beautiful scene. Pastor Charles had made special arrangements to house me there. He urged me to take a walk with him in order to drink in the beauty. When he later learned how poorly I was feeling, he apologized many times. No apology was necessary. He was demonstrating the gentility of an extraordinary city.

In this extraordinary city, the St. Andrews Church of the Nazarene must be one of the most remarkable. Not for its size: about one hundred persons gather each Lord's Day morning. Nor its architecture: it is a very pleasantly kept but modest sanctuary to accommodate about 250 persons, located on Ashley Hall Road. It does not compete with the tall steeples of the "historic area."

St. Andrews is extraordinary in its racial and cultural mix and diversity. It illustrates the unity in Christ that persons of diverse culture can know.

As one might expect, there are several long-term resident Anglo-Southerners who have worked hard and with success in a variety of trades. But there is a larger number of persons with various other backgrounds: people whose ancestors came from the Caribbean Islands many years ago and recent immigrants from the European, African, and Asian continents. AND THEY ALL GET ALONG AS CHRISTIAN BROTHERS AND SISTERS OUGHT TO GET ALONG. I mean, in the heart of the Deep South, with all that is implied by that description, brothers and sisters have been able to focus on what they have in common in Jesus Christ rather than what they have as differences.

At a recent service in which they celebrated their diversity, there were eight culture and language groups represented. People are granted leadership roles because of their gifts and graces rather than because of the color of their skin, their gender, or their cultural origin. And there are no "token representatives."

Their youth group musical ensemble is delightful to hear and watch. They do "move" and the music does have a "rhythm," but you cannot tell whether it is an African harmony, a Caribbean tempo, or a Dixieland beat. One gets the feeling that all of them are in there somewhere, and the combination is music to the ears.

This kind of harmony in diversity is possible only by the sanctifying grace of the Holy Spirit bestowed on the people. The leading human factors are Pastor Fountain and his wife, Louise, who served for six years as missionaries in Panama, Barbados in the West Indies, and the Philippines. They propagate and experience the brotherhood of man in many practical ways.

Along with the pastor is the key leadership of the church that includes Brother Bob Pelham. He has spent his life in the South as a successful Anglo roofing contractor. But he and his wife, Bell, see their love for Christ as the basis of their love for all of His people, regardless of race and culture.

Four Afro-American doctors and their spouses round out this circle of grace in leadership that makes this special church possible.

Brother Bob was the one who discovered at the Sunday dinner that something was wrong with me. He called Dr. Hazell and Dr. Rashford to my side and they began to look me over. Dr. Hazell is chief of surgery at the St. Francis Hospital, and Dr. Rashford is the cardiopulmonary specialist at the Roper Hospital. He had had an emergency call that very morning and had knelt at the altar in the morning service in order to be anointed by me on behalf of that patient. Little did either of us know that I would soon be his patient.

These two doctors agreed between themselves that Dr. Rashford would take me to the Roper Hospital for possible admittance. When he and I entered the emergency room, everyone moved quickly to accommodate this highly respected doctor and his "special patient."

Throughout Sunday evening and Monday morning, he remained my doctor of record. But by midday Monday, I was losing consciousness, and he extended the team to try to gain a diagnosis of my problem.

My recollections of Drs. Hazell and Rashford are very fragmented from that time forward. But they are very precious memories. Sometime—I do not know whether it was before or after I was transferred to the Medical Center for the University of South Carolina—I remember their coming to my side. My best sense was that I was in a medical intensive care unit. Dr. Hazell greeted me warmly and told me he realized I was not feeling well. That assessment was certainly true. And then Dr. Rashford explained to me that he and Dr. Hazell had done what they could do and that they had had to pass me along to specialists who had more experience with my problem. I nodded my consent.

But then Dr. Rashford said, "We are no longer your doctors, but we are still your brothers, and we want to hold you up to our Heavenly Father in prayer." Then in earnestness, they hovered over my gurney and began to pray the sweetest prayer I may ever hope to feel. I say "feel" because I do not sense that I understood the words even at that time. I certainly do not remember them now. I wish I could. But I do remember what I felt. I felt the power of the blessed Holy Spirit and the fellowship of two precious brothers in the Lord.

And it was somehow all the more wonderful to know that precious unity in prayer was taking place right here in Charleston.

This hospital, where these men are chief administrators, is just minutes from the old slave market where four generations ago black men and women were sold as chattel. Now these two men, who share that lineage, are laying claim to the words of Scripture that call us to be "brothers in the faith, incorporate in Christ" (Col.1:2). As members of the holy "corporation," they were laying claim to the resources of Christ on my behalf. What a wonderful experience for me! I am very glad that, among the brief memories that I can salvage from that week, I can recall being prayed for by these good doctors.

Later in the week my family arrived, still believing that my only chance for survival was a transplant. With this prognosis in mind, Dr. Rashford offered to let my entire family live with him and his family during my hospitalization. And Brother Bob offered his family's summer home on Kiawah for the anticipated months of recovery.

A city that was a market of racial oppression for nearly a century and was the symbol of national division for nearly as long became a testimony of fraternity, restoration, and healing for me.

I will always remember that "the king's city" is really THE KING'S CITY.

◆ ⠶ ⠶ ◆ ⠶◗◖⠶ ◆ ⠶ ⠶ ◆

Discoveries on the Way

Each member of the family of God is important. The greater the diversity, the greater the range of service that may be rendered by one member of the family to any other.

What would I have done had Bob not asked about me or if Drs. Hazell and Rashford not been present in the service?

I will continue to learn how essential each member of the household of faith is and, consequently, how precious each is!

Chapter 4
Words from "The Book"

The Lord will protect him and preserve his life; he will bless him in the land and not surrender him to the desire of his foes. The Lord will sustain him on his sickbed and restore him from his bed of illness.
Psalm 41:2-3 (NIV)

John Wesley spoke of himself as "a man of one book." As a "son of Wesley," I often point out that he never intended that statement to keep us from reading many good books. He was, himself, an avid reader of the apostolic fathers as well as a rich variety of writers contemporary to his time. What he was saying and what I affirm is this: There is one book that has no peer or comparison. It is the Bible, "by which we understand the sixty-six books of the Old and New Testaments, given by divine inspiration, inerrantly revealing the will of God concerning us in all things necessary to our salvation" (from the early Methodist Confession of Faith).

> *I am in awe at the power of the Scripture and the skill of the Spirit in searching it out and applying it to the heart of the needy believer.*

Two portions of Scripture spoke to me like the very voice of God during my sickness, healing, and recovery. I cannot share my story without including them.

COLOSSIANS

The first portion of Scripture that was so "alive" to me throughout this experience is the book of Colossians. When I was invited to lead this extraordinary congregation in South Carolina in four consecutive enrichment services over a weekend, my prayer time went toward the question, "Oh Lord, what portion of your Word do you want me to bring to the hearts of your people?"

After several conversations with Pastor Fountain and more reflection and prayer, I was led to the wonderful brief letter of Paul to the people of Colossae.

The pastor had spoken warmly of his people, much as a father would of his children. I had always felt that Colossians was a letter to Paul's "spiritual grandchildren." He had not been there, but his son in the Lord, Epaphras, was their spiritual father. Notice how the letter fairly glows with grandfatherly pride.

Colossians 1:3-8:
In all our prayers to God, the Father of our Lord Jesus Christ, we thank him for you, because we have heard of the FAITH you hold in Christ Jesus, and the LOVE you bear towards all God's people. Both spring from the HOPE stored up for you in heaven—that hope of which you learned when the message of the true Gospel first came to you. In the same way it is coming to men the whole world over; everywhere it is growing and bearing fruit as it does among you, and has done since the day when you heard of the graciousness of God and recognized it for what in truth it is. You were taught this by Epaphras, our dear fellow-servant, a trusted worker for Christ on our behalf, and it is he who has brought us the news of your God-given love.

When I first read this paragraph from Colossians in anticipation of the St. Andrews meeting, I thought, "That is it! Look at the joy Paul has in this congregation. Notice the international flavor. Maybe I can even fill the role of surrogate 'spiritual grandfather.' I do not know these people, but I know Pastor Fountain and feel as if I know them through him." I was also impressed with the way this brief passage provided an insight into the personality and the theology of the apostle. In the first four lines are the three qualities that he enlarges on in his Corinthian letter as being "abiding qualities"— "faith, hope, and love." My heart was at ease. Colossians would be God's Word for his people at St. Andrews. I did not realize that this Scripture would come to have special application to my personal crisis time as well.

I have already quoted from Colossians in earlier chapters. As you read the following chapters you will see how, time after time, a phrase from this brief letter applied to my situation precisely.

PSALM 41:2-3
During the weeks that I stayed home while regaining strength, I enjoyed many letters from friends. Often they would include a promise or word of encouragement from the Scripture. I enjoyed them all, but one affixed itself to my heart in a special way and

taught me a new lesson on how precisely the Holy Spirit applies a passage to the heart of a believer.

I had known John and Carol Hadlock for a number of years as "fellow pastors." So I was pleased to see an envelope with their return address. Their note recounted how they had heard of my sickness and how they went immediately to their "prayer room" determined to stay there until the Lord gave them a passage especially for their "Brother Millard."

After some hours, they came upon Psalm 41, verses two and three. They copied it for me from the *New International Version:* "The Lord will protect him and preserve his life; he will bless him in the land and not surrender him to the desire of his foes. The Lord will sustain him on his sickbed and restore him from his bed of illness."

I couldn't believe that I was not already familiar with that passage. I had visited and prayed for the sick for many years, but I had never seen, never really seen, this passage. I accepted it as a "fresh word" from God and called my wife to read it to her in order that we could rejoice together.

After reading the passage, I did comment, "Of course, that part about my 'foes' just doesn't apply to me. We have been treated well through all the years and been loved beyond what we deserve. I claim the first part and the last part. Two parts out of three are not bad." I wasn't flippant. I was just grateful for how kindly I had always been treated.

I can almost hear some of you who are experienced in the things of the Lord and the strategy of the devil run ahead of me in this story. **The very Sunday I was taken ill**, a person sent me a letter accusing me of sexual discrimination and harassment. **The very week I was lying near death**, a handful of former employees and students gathered addresses in order to activate a scandalous letter campaign against me.

In light of my dire illness, my secretary opened my mail, including my private mail. When she came across the letter of accusation with threats to take legal action if the accuser was not generously compensated, she shared it with our dean who had already assumed official leadership of the school because of my illness. He shared it with the President's Cabinet immediately.

Bless my dear Cabinet! I was off in South Carolina, and they were not sure that I would live through the week. They wondered what they should do. They decided to hold steady for a few days until I was out of the hospital. With my miraculous recovery, they decided to keep the accusations from me until I returned to take the authority of leadership again. We still laugh about my first meeting with them. In each case I asked, "And how are things in the academic area? Student affairs? Recruitment? Finances? In every case, my administrators assured me that everything was "just fine." Later they admitted, "We were not about to tell you anything but good news."

Since I was to reassume the leadership of the University on May first, I began having brief daily meetings with Dean Pusey by the third week of April. Near the first of May, we were in one of those meetings. With some discomfort, he said, "There is one matter I need to let you know about." "What is that?" I responded. "We have been threatened with a lawsuit for sexual discrimination and sexual harassment." My first response was "Whom is the charge against?" That question must have made Dr. Pusey feel much like Nathan with King David when Nathan said, "Thou art the man!" Dr. Pusey responded, "The charge is against you."

I was absolutely nonplussed. I had grown accustomed to our litigious society and had come to know that universities are most susceptible to charges that spring from financial motives, but I had no hint about any charge against me. I had enjoyed a long pastoral career without a shadow of accusation. I really felt that I had no "foes." People who disagreed with me? Sure! Church members unhappy with me? From time to time! An occasional vote against me at re-election time? You bet! But foes? Never foes!

As you would expect, I shared this disheartening news with Barbara when I went home that afternoon. After I had explained as much as I knew about it and after we had had time to think, we prayed. Then she said, "All three parts of your promise from Psalm 41 apply to you. You didn't know it back in March, but God knew it and He sent His Word then so that you could be encouraged now."

The attack was painful for me. I had never experienced false accusation like that before. Further details would fill no positive purpose here. I am pleased to assure you, however, that the Lord keeps His promise and that "the desire of [my] foes" was in no degree realized against me.

Never had a Scripture applied so accurately and so fully to me. I am in awe at the power of the Scripture and the skill of the Spirit in searching it out and applying it to the heart of the needy believer.

As you continue through this story, I hope you will gain a deeper appreciation for Paul's letter to the Colossians as well as for these two brief verses from Psalm 41.

* ‧ ‡‧ ❧◗❀◖❧ ‡‧ ‧ *

Discoveries on the Way

God delivers His Word to us with a personal precision and in a timely manner. The fact that we often do not at first recognize it does not lessen the truth. And from time to time, He delivers it in such a dramatic way that we cannot deny its validity.

I will read the Word often with a sensitivity to catch any message He may have for me or for another. And I will be open to receive a word that another may have discovered for me.

Chapter 5

Trusted Workers for Christ on My Behalf

Our dear fellow-servant, a trusted worker for Christ on our behalf. . .
Colossians 1:8 (NEB)

Within two hours of my admittance to the Roper Hospital, Dr. Melvin Welch, dean of the Division of Education at Trevecca and my administrative assistant, was at my bedside.

He had been driving all day from Nashville in order to be at his father's side for a surgery scheduled for Tuesday morning. It "happened" that his parents live in Charleston and that the surgery was scheduled for the Roper Hospital. Coincidence! Right? Hardly!

> *I really do believe that God gives "dying grace."*

By the time Melvin arrived at his parents' home, they had learned of my illness, and his father met him in the driveway to urge him to "get on down to the hospital." "Can't I at least go to the bathroom? Say hello to Mom?" "No, Dr. Reed needs you!" And Mom waved him on from the door. Melvin was soon at my side. He is the first of several "dear fellow servants" who became "trusted workers for Christ on my behalf" in the weeks that followed. I can mention only a few.

It was good to have a friend at my side through that Sunday evening. I was still treating my illness casually. I called my wife, Barbara, but assured her that my condition was probably not serious and suggested that she not worry the children with a call. When the evening wore on and a diagnosis seemed slow in coming, I gave the medical team the "advantage" of my years of experience as a pastor and pointed out that often when diagnosis is difficult, the problem has to do with the gall bladder. The doctors thanked me for my help. Somehow, I didn't think they were sincere.

It was late in the night before the specialist left me. In fact, I am not sure if I slept or was otherwise unconscious Sunday night. I know that my memories of Monday are fragmentary.

I do remember a sweet, teenage candy striper who must have drawn me as her first assignment. She entered my room with the bubbly enthusiasm of a "bobbin' red robin." "Hello, Mr. Reed! I am Tiffany and I am here to cheer you up today. We can talk together. I can even go with you down to the examining room and we can chat there, too." She was still cheery and waiting for my equally cheerful response.

"Oh, no, dear. Please, I really don't want to talk to anybody!" I said. She soon disappeared and I have no recollection of her coming back. I hope I did not abort what might otherwise have been a long and brilliant career in nursing.

Pastor Fountain came by. I sensed that he was deeply concerned for me. He and Melvin had gotten my things from the lovely Middleton Gardens Inn. As I remember, he did not stay long. But I clearly remember that he prayed for me. How sweet the spirit of his prayer! For more than thirty-five years, I had prayed brief prayers at hospital bedsides. I had NEVER been in the bed as someone else prayed. Only there could I learn the precious value of a pastoral prayer.

As I had left the church on Sunday afternoon, I had asked Pastor Fountain to tell Stan and Kathy Parker that their "precious, old pastor was in the hospital and would love to see their smiling faces." They had attended Trevecca, had been a part of the church I pastored in Nashville, and were now pastors of their own congregation in Charleston.

Sometime Monday afternoon, Kathy came by to see me. I remember very little about the visit except that she told me that Stan was out of the city and would be back the next day. And I remembered how wonderfully beautiful Kathy was. She radiated an aura that would enhance several faces before my recovery was complete. I will tell more of her visit in the following chapter.

I don't really remember Bob Pelham's coming by. He wrote me later: "I visited you the next day at the hospital. I got so upset and knew that God would have to intervene and heal you. The doctors said that you would need a liver transplant."

To this day, I do not remember the doctors' ever telling me that I had hepatitis A, nor that it had gone "fulminant." I do recall that they mentioned a liver transplant, and I remember asking, "Do you mean that someone must die if I am to live?" I also remember calling Barbara late Monday night with Melvin's help and telling her I "might need" a transplant. My situation did not seem serious to me somehow. But Barbara was shocked. She seemed to want to get through those telephone lines to be at my side. Lacking that ability, she pressed to help me in some way. "Is there anything I can do for you?" she asked. "Can I call someone?" As sick as I was, a tinge of mischief made its way through my mind. She has two tiny dogs that are the joy of her life and the bane of mine. They are a constant joke between us. "My children, your dogs!" I would often say. But when she asked me if she could help, I feigned a voice that was even weaker than it already was and said, "No, just take care of my little puppy dogs, especially Sweetie!" I still wonder at the processes of the semiconscious mind.

Tuesday was bad. Poor Melvin was drawn in all directions. His father would soon be under the surgeon's knife, and I was encephalopathic (a word the doctors gave me later to describe the condition of one who is engaging in partially rational conversations but is left with no memory of them). My family had not yet arrived. Word from the doctor was very bad. Concerned phone calls were coming in from the College and the church. Melvin also needed to attend to his father whose surgery time was just minutes away.

Just at the last possible moment, "pastor son" Stan Parker walked in. "Oh, thank the Lord! Here, attend to him," said Melvin, "I must be with my father." Later Stan told me, "Your face was blood red when I walked into your room, and you were so hot to the touch, that I can't imagine your temperature reading." (Later doctors told me it was around 105 degrees much of the week.) "I moved quickly to put cold cloths on your face, but they seemed to become warm quicker than I could replace them. Then you began to throw up clear, thick liquid. I rang for help but the nurses took a while getting to you. While I was in the middle of all the mess, the phone rang and someone identified himself from the information office for the worldwide Church of the Nazarene in Kansas City." "Can you give us a report on Dr. Reed's condition, please?" "No, I really can't! I said, I am too busy." I have only the vaguest memory of Stan's being there. I am told by Melvin and my family that he attended to me through those first days. He was a "dear fellow-servant, a trusted worker for Christ on my behalf."

Sometime Tuesday I was transferred to the Medical Center of the University of South Carolina. Although it was a part of the same medical complex, this change of location made the shuffle more difficult for Melvin.

Now the diagnosis was precise. "Viral pneumonia with fulminant hepatic failure. This latter condition causes the rapid destruction of the liver cells. The patient must have a transplant to survive" (Rashford). All doctors were in agreement. They differed only in the number of days they speculated were mine for such a transplant. Some said as few as six days. Others more optimistically gave me eleven. I had taken on that deep golden color that characterizes patients with liver degeneration, and my stomach was swelling as a woman's does when she is with child.

I know this sounds silly, but I feel so bad that I was not there to help Melvin. I know I was there. I was the center of his interest. But I was not truly there to assist in any way. I know he must have felt great pressure in trying to attend to his father, attend to me, communicate with the College and the church, AND assist my family as they were trying desperately to get to Charleston.

I do have one faint memory that he tells me took place on that Tuesday evening. I remember sensing that I would probably die. I have no memory of anyone's telling me that I would, but I sensed it to be so. I was not distressed by that fact. I remember musing, "I am a little young. My father died at fifty-eight; Barbara's dad, at sixty-four. Sixty-two is a little young, but I have lived a good life." I really do believe that God gives "dying grace."

I had little sense of time but was aware that Melvin might have to leave me soon. "Before you go," I said to him, "let me talk to you. It looks like my situation may go bad. It could be that I would not make it for my family's arrival. Please let me leave my testimony with you for them."

I remember concentrating so intensely in order that I might say just the right thing. I sensed my "dear fellow-servant" leaning in to hear me, concentrating as hard as I so that he might repeat to my family accurately should I never get the opportunity. As the words began to flow, they took the form of the Apostle's Creed. Melvin tells me I took a little liberty with it but basically he heard, "I believe in God the Father almighty, maker of heaven and earth, and in Jesus Christ His Son our Lord who was conceived of the Holy Ghost, born of the Virgin Mary, suffered under Pontius Pilate, was crucified, dead, and buried; the third day he arose from the grave. . . ."

At that point, I do remember pleading the blood of Jesus Christ as the atonement for my sins and my hope of heaven.

Many theologians of our Wesleyan holiness tradition maintain that the Scripture is very clear that the human heart is truly cleansed in the experience of entire sanctification. To my knowledge, only E. Stanley Jones, the beloved missionary to India and Spirit-anointed writer, maintains that the subconscious is also cleansed. Most concede, by the evidence of devious dreams and nonvolitional thoughts, that the subconscious is not cleansed.

I am inclined to think that the conversation may not be a legitimate one since it mixes theological and psychological terminology and thoughts. But I am fascinated by the deep confessional aspect of my semiconscious mind. I am comforted to know that the truths of our faith have sunk deeply into my awareness, either consciously or unconsciously.

🦎   🦎   🦎

Another couple who are my "dear fellow-servants" are Fred and Dinah Huff. They had been youth ministers in my church in Nashville. Then, when they went off to the mission field, Barbara and I visited them as our church built chapels where they were. I dedicated their children. I was a friend of Dinah's dad and was there for his funeral. I think she has let me fill some of his place in her life. For four years Fred had served Trevecca as vice president for church relations, and they were in South Carolina for a pastors' retreat when I became ill. By Wednesday, they were at my side. Dinah tells me that I told her that I had nearly "left them" twice that day. I have no memory of anything that would have caused me to say that.

I do have one brief memory of Fred. Unlike these other stories that affirm my confidence in the deep work of the Spirit to saturate every aspect of one's psyche, this memory demonstrates the penetrating effect of contemporary marketing. It was time for Fred and Dinah to go, and both of them were deeply worried. The raspy voice with which I responded to them reminded Dinah of her father's voice shortly before his death.

I remember Fred's leaning over me and saying earnestly, "We will be praying for you!" Then he added, "I love you, man!" With that raspy voice I responded, "Sounds like a Budweiser commercial to me!" As they walked out he was saying, "Surely he is going to be O.K!" I remember that episode and recall thinking I was funny— another curious thing about the encephalopathic mind.

Other "dear fellow-servants" who were "trusted workers for Christ on [my] behalf" came. Dr. Jim Bearden, superintendent of the South Carolina District and my dear friend, came. I have only a fleeting memory of him. Others came (whom I do not recall) who are no less dear. Steve and Connie Callis, who pastor in Columbia, came. They say I said, "Look who has come to see me" and asked them to pray for me. I was the first one to whom he ever confided his call to preach. I dedicated their children, Mandie and Kevin. Kevin Ulmet came down from Greenville. I had been his pastor while he was in college and like to think I am something of a mentor for his ministry today.

How can I adequately express my deep appreciation to these dear friends? Each served me unselfishly. I loved each of them before. I love each of them more deeply now. All of them are "dear fellow-servants" and trusted worker[s] "for Christ ON MY BEHALF."

Discoveries on the Way

While I esteem all the members of the family of God, I recognize that God has placed some very close to me in order that He may provide His loving service to me through them.

I recognize that, in this divine order of things, the affection is mutual so that both they and I are blessed in the relationship of mutual service.

I resolve to cherish these servants from the Lord even more affectionately and look for ways in which I may serve them and others.

Chapter 6
A Campus Prays

For this reason, ever since the day we heard of it, we have not ceased to pray for you. We ask God that you may receive from him all wisdom and spiritual understanding for full insight into his will, so that your manner of life may be worthy of the Lord and entirely pleasing to him. We pray that you may bear fruit in active goodness of every kind, and grow in the knowledge of God.

Colossians 1:9-10 (NEB)

From the day I came to lead Trevecca, this brief paragraph had been my prayer for the College. Phrases like "wisdom and spiritual understanding," "full insight into his will," and "a manner of life...worthy of the Lord and entirely pleasing to him" have often been the focus of my chapel messages. I had always known that a primary duty of the president of a holiness college was to pray for his students, faculty, and administration. It had never quite occurred to me that it is also the privilege of students, faculty, and administrators to pray for their president.

Who can assess the power of prayer? I do not believe it is our task to make quantitative measurements of prayer.

The word of my hospitalization arrived on campus Monday morning, but most members of the College family accepted my assessment that "it is not serious." Because everyone knew that I had had excellent health, concern was minimal. Tuesday was a different thing. With the message "liver transplant necessary for survival," the campus, I am told, sprang into action.

A policy was in place that calls for the academic vice president to assume the role of chief operational officer in the event the president is incapacitated or dies. The President's Cabinet met to discuss my situation, and, with. the endorsement of the chairman of the Board of Trustees, Dean Pusey assumed the authority of my office. That explains the "business side of it."

Chaplain Tim Green sent me this brief report regarding the more important "spiritual" side of it:

When we learned how serious Dr. Reed was, we knew we had to inform the students. Dr. Pusey and I discussed how we should present the seriousness of the situation. We were in full agreement that the one setting in which our entire community had grown accustomed to celebrating the grace of God together in worship would be most appropriate—the morning chapel. Amazingly, the theme of the morning service (planned three months in advance) was experiencing the "optimism of God's grace" in the unexpected turns of life.

Following a brief time of worship through music and an abbreviated message concerning the optimism of God's grace in those unexpected turns, Dr. Pusey read a formal statement concerning President Reed's situation. I will never forget the looks of fear, anxiety, and dismay that permeated that chapel auditorium, from students to faculty to staff to administrators. Dr. Reed was the one to whom we had all looked for vision, strength, encouragement, and—yes—prayer.

At first a sense of "helplessness" seemed to spread across the auditorium; however, as I came back to the pulpit and before I could finish with further remarks, persons from all over the auditorium began to make their way to the altar. Students whom I had never seen bow at an altar before came to kneel before the presence of the Great Physician. In a matter of a couple minutes, the pews had nearly emptied and together the community truly came to recognize what it meant to be utterly dependent upon the optimism of God's grace. The great diversity of our University campus now gave breath to one common voice as our hearts joined in prayer that morning.

Throughout the day, persons remained in the chapel praying. While others made their way to classes or the cafeteria, spontaneous prayer times broke out both in classrooms and around cafeteria tables.

Throughout the following days, I would often pass by the chapel or enter into the prayer chapel and find individuals or small groups in prayer. Groups in dormitories organized to devote concerted prayer to the matter; special prayer times were organized throughout the day in various locations and by various groups. The atmosphere which permeated the very air of the campus became an atmosphere of prayer—not a prayer in which the Trevecca community attempted to "strong arm" God into healing our beloved president, but a prayer which recognized our utter dependence upon God's grace. Amazingly, we discovered truly what it meant for us to be "community" in the midst of our diversity as we found our oneness in our trust and dependence upon God.

Who can assess the power of the prayer of some fifteen hundred students? I do not believe that it is our task to make quantitative measurements of prayer, but my heart is blessed, even now, to think of students, faculty, and administration on their knees before the Lord in prayer for me.

I have tried to imagine the mood of the campus during that week. Of course, I cannot. It is our tradition at Trevecca to open every class session with prayer. I am told that from class to class throughout the day and evening classes, each class inquired of any progress I may have made and went again to the Heavenly Father in prayer for me. Tuesday, Wednesday, and Thursday were gloomy days on campus, I am told.

Marvin Jones, who is minister of music at the College Hill Church of the Nazarene and one of our music students, shared a story that illustrates some of the concern of the campus: "My wife, Paula, and I had been with our folks back East when we learned how seriously ill Dr. Reed was. As we were driving back toward Nashville, we kept him in our prayers. As we pulled onto the campus, I saw that the flags were flying at half-mast. I WENT BALLISTIC! I went dashing from building to building to see if someone could tell me whether the president was dead or not."

(The flags were flying at half-mast in honor of a true friend of the college, Ms. Sarah Cannon, known to the world as the beloved country comedienne, Minnie Pearl.)

Someone had the idea of making a "Blessing Banner" for me. I have been known for pointing out that the Scripture is filled with blessings that we Christians ought to use on one another—that we all need to be "blessed" by our fellow Christians. Students remembered my saying, "The only sure way to be blessed these days is to sneeze. If you sneeze, someone will say 'Bless you!'"

A long, paper banner was set up on the Student Union Building, and students gathered around to send me some greeting, some assurance of their prayers. The banner is now a cherished treasure for me. It contains hundreds of "blessings" from students who I believe are going to "bless" and enrich their world. Here are a few of those messages:

"Grace and Peace to you, my friend, mentor, and fraternal brother. With love, Jason Vickers"

"I really miss you! I hope you get better really soon! I will be praying for you and I expect a big hug when you get back. Tell Mrs. Reed that she is in my prayers as well! I love you! Laura Hall"

"May the grace of the Lord our God be with your spirit as you heal. Mitchel Modine"

"Remembering you in prayers and that we miss you. Get well! God Bless, Stacy Calton"

"You are a wonderful man. We need you here at Trevecca. No one else is able to fill your place, so get better. I'm praying for you. I pray that the Holy Spirit be ever so close to you. Love, Hannah Kisner"

"We are praying for God's peace to be known to you in a special way. Mark and Janet Chitty"

"We love you and are praying for you. Be still and know that God is always with you. Get well soon. Love in the Anointing. Carolyn Stewart"

"I love ya man!! My prayers are for you. Wayne!!"

"You are in our thoughts and prayers constantly. All of us love you and look forward to seeing your smiling face again. Love and prayers, Lori McVay"

"You are in all our prayers and thoughts. I can't wait to see you walking around campus again. We miss you a lot, and we love you! Love, LeAnn Neely"

"God has purposed your life in a very special way and in his plan, everything works out for those who trust the Lord. Connie L."

"Now it is our turn to give back to you...Kenneth Couchman"

"Dr. Reed: God Bless, We're prayin' for you. See ya soon, Ace Wimbly"

(I especially wanted to include Ace Wimbly's note. As I was getting well, Ace was getting sick. He died of cancer November 4, 1996. I want to say to him what he said to me: "I'll see ya soon, Ace.")

My first public time back on campus was on March 19, 1996, just twelve days after I had been dismissed from the hospital. It was the spring Board of Trustees meeting and it was a special occasion. The "College" was to officially become "University" on that day. I was still very yellow, and my weight loss of nearly twenty pounds was very obvious.

But I was so happy to be alive, and I wanted to see my students. Maybe I wanted them to see me and know that God answers prayer. I asked Dean Pusey to read my address which I had completed before going to South Carolina. Then I inquired of my doctor about the possibility of my opening the Convocation with a call to worship and a brief testimony of God's healing grace on my behalf. A total of six or seven minutes, maximum! Barbara said no. But Dr. Burk said yes. I accepted Dr. Burk's word.

I led the academic procession as it was my duty to do and took my place on the platform as the wonderful faculty and administrators filed in. They were beautiful! I learned later that they had placed our campus medical doctor, Dr. Moredock, just behind me in line to attend to me in the event I pitched over.

God helped me. I made the call to worship with my still raspy voice, and then I thanked them for their prayers and told them of my healing. At the close of our six minutes together, I shared with them how a song had come to me in intensive care the first night after I regained consciousness. I acknowledged to them that I had sung it out loud back then and wanted to sing it with them now. I sang it through and then they all joined me as we repeated it: "I sing praises to your name, Oh Lord! Praises to your name, Oh Lord! For your name is great and greatly to be praised."

I had promised Barbara that that short presentation would be as much as I would do. So while the great chapel audience of campus personnel continued to sing His praises, she and I walked out the center aisle. How fortunate we were to have that great army of young people praying for us.

Discoveries on the Way

Maturity is not a matter of years. It is a matter of growth in the Spirit of Christ.

As a young man, I turned down an invitation to spend a lifetime in Christian higher education. I declined, concluding that I did not want to spend my life serving adolescents exclusively.

Through the years, I have learned that many young people are very mature in spirit.

I thank God for my young friends who held me up to the Heavenly Father in prayer. I aspire to become as mature in the Spirit as they are.

Chapter 7

The Church Grapevine

We pray that you'll have the strength to stick it out over the long haul—not the grim strength of gritting your teeth but the glory-strength God gives. It is strength that endures the unendurable and spills over into joy, thanking the Father who makes us strong enough to take part in everything bright and beautiful that he has for us.
                              Colossians 1:10-11 *(The Message)*

From time to time I hear complaints about the "church grapevine." Someone will say, "There is no privacy around the church. Everybody knows everything about everything and everybody once news is on the 'church grapevine.'" I have been inclined to agree with the complainer upon occasion when it seemed that my life was pretty much lived in a "glass fishbowl."

But since the first Sunday of March 1996, I have thanked God for the "church grapevine." Count me in. I do not want to be left out.

It has seemed to me that the Lord himself had arranged for a series of "prayer cells along the grapevine" through the eight days of my unconsciousness.

> *How wonderful is the "family of God"! It surrounds the world and counts its children in every affiliation and fellowship.*

I mentioned Fred and Dinah Huff earlier. They were in a pastor's retreat in nearby Myrtle Beach. By a routine call back to campus, Fred learned that I was hospitalized, so he made a call to Charleston, assuming that my case was not serious. When he got the fresh word that without a liver transplant I would die, he went back into the morning preaching session where Dr. Jerry Porter had begun to preach. Fred was not to be deterred by a sermon in progress. He interrupted the message to inform a hundred or so pastors and wives that their friend Millard was in trouble and needed their prayers. Dr. Porter said, "There is no better time than now." The morning sermon waited while that "prayer cell" prayed for me. Steve Callis, a "pastor son" in South Carolina was asked to lead the prayer.

A regional senior adult retreat had just convened in Lake Yale, Florida. Participants got word on the "grapevine" and prayed for me.

A great regional gathering of Sunday school folks were gathered in Indianapolis for a conference called "Improve Your Serve!" Pastor Jan Forman had developed that format and title while on staff with me in Nashville First Church. He and I had written a book on Sunday school with that title. When those attending the conference learned of my condition, they became a "prayer cell" on my behalf.

The General Board of the Church of the Nazarene meets for three days each year. I was to have been at this board's yearly meeting. Representatives from all over the world were there for the plenary sessions. They, of course, assumed that they were there to do business for the Church, and I suppose that was the case. The "grapevine" carried the news of my serious illness to that meeting, and the group prayed for me. By this method the "grapevine" reached all around the world. I was happy to be in on it.

At this same meeting the six leaders of the church were in private session with careful instruction that they were not to be disturbed. But when the wife of one of the men heard the details, like Esther of old, she entered into the "throne room." Of course, these good men were eager to change the agenda of the meeting and paused to pray for their brother in Christ.

The reach of this "international grapevine" is further illustrated by what happened to a fine team of church people from Tennessee who had just made their way to northern Thailand to build a chapel. One of those half-way-around-the-world telephone calls informed them of my sickness. I am saying, "I like this grapevine!"

During the same crucial week the presidents of private colleges in the State of Tennessee were in conference. Since I had expected to be in Kansas City for the general meetings of the Church of the Nazarene, I had asked our director of development, Mr. Harold McCue, to represent me at these meetings. As they convened on Wednesday morning, Harold informed them of my life-threatening situation. The presidents of the private colleges in the State of Tennessee made a place at the top of their agenda to pray for one of their brothers—another "prayer cell."

It "happened" that the Church Board of the First Church of the Nazarene in Nashville was to meet on that Wednesday evening. Since I had served with these dear brothers and sisters for some seventeen years, the love ties are very precious. Some had heard of my illness but most had not been informed of how serious it was.

Pastor Gary Henecke had been told shortly before the meeting. Again, prayer became the priority. Gerald Skinner, a dear brother to me who had been a great help in my early days at the College as well as through the years at the church, was designated to represent me at the prayer time. I am told that the others gathered around, laid their hands upon Gerald, and prayed earnestly for my recovery.

Many of the "prayer cells" were within the Church of the Nazarene since I have spent my life in that denomination. But this great prayer network is not limited to my denomination. My "little sister," Martha Garvin, who has a nation-wide television ministry called "Musical Memories," told me this story in a letter:

> When we arrived in Quincy, I called again and was told that your enzyme count was over 9000. I was also told it should be in the 50s. When I informed Marvin [our brother], his face turned ashen. I know he tried to keep me from knowing how grave your situation was but with his background in medicine he could not disguise it. About that time, [Martha's nurse-daughter] Lorri called from Nashville to inform us that an enzyme count of 9000 is "total liver failure."

> Thursday morning dawned and the news was still not good, but I decided to go ahead and tape my programs as planned. I walked bravely into the studio with my music in hand, thinking that I had my emotions pretty well under control. But the first person I saw was the owner of the station, a dear friend and a man of God. My control crumbled as I tried to tell him between deep and repeated sobs how desperately ill you were. The station personnel remembered you since you had recently recorded with me, singing such wonderful old songs as "Take the Name of Jesus with You" and "There's No Disappointment in Heaven." They had been blessed as we had sung these old favorites of our parents.

> Thank goodness for automatic controls at Channel 16! Everyone except one engineer gathered around me and a volume of prayer started to ascend to the Father. Many hands were raised to heaven as we prayed on that Thursday morning.

> When the spontaneous prayer meeting was ended, I dried my tears and started recording. The first song was "It

Is Well with My Soul." I made it through without breaking down. I think some of them must have prayed for me too. At the conclusion of the recording session, I was amused at the owner when he said, "You Nazarenes surely are gutsy."

Maybe all of these prayer cells were coincidences, collisions of schedules that just happened to coincide with the crucial days of my struggle for life. Those who refuse to be convinced of the providence of prayer may not be convinced by a coincidence of schedules. But those of us who are familiar with the "church grapevine" know better. We have been impressed to pray for a friend and learned later of our friend's critical need just at that time. And we have also been on the receiving end of such God-prompted prayer. I like being "on the grapevine."

The story that I most enjoy about the "vine" is one that I learned several weeks later. It was late April, and I had begun to carry out a few of my duties. My doctor approved a brief trip to Mississippi where I was to be the guest of District Superintendent Rev. Roy Rogers and the people of Mississippi. On my return flight to Nashville, I was to stop in Atlanta. (Word in the South is that one cannot go to heaven or the other place unless one goes through Atlanta.)

Barbara had worried about my making it from gate to gate and so, without my knowledge, called Pastor Ed Husband in Atlanta and asked if he would meet me and assist me. I was a bit embarrassed that my good brother would have to come out to a busy airport for this sweet service, but I was happy for his help and got to chat with him for a while.

As we visited, he inquired about my health, and I was happy to tell him the story of my miraculous recovery. As we talked, I noticed that a pleasant young woman, across the waiting room from us, seemed to be leaning in to hear the details of our conversation. Finally, she approached us with a cordial smile and asked me, "Are you the president of a church college in Nashville?" "Well, yes, I am," I responded. "Why do you ask?" "I think I have been praying for you for the last five weeks!" "That news sounds wonderfully right to me!" I said, "But how do you know me?" "Well, I really don't. I wasn't sure of your name or the college that you serve. But I am a part of a Church of Christ congregation in Nashville, and my Sunday school teacher is finishing a degree at Trevecca. Over the last five weeks he has mentioned you each time we meet. I have been praying for you faithfully."

How wonderful is the "family of God"! It surrounds the world and counts its children in every affiliation and fellowship. I have nothing bad to say about the "grapevine!" I am just glad I have been and am a part of it.

＊

Discoveries on the Way

Networks are as good and beneficial as the persons who share them are.

We have learned that the Internet can be a great blessing or an insidious defiler of the mind.

The "Worldwide Web" was not first devised by the clever genius of the computer buffs. The first "Worldwide Web" was what Jesus had in mind when He said, "Go and make disciples of all nations" (Matt. 28:19).

I will "surf the 'Net" in spiritual matters to learn whom I may assist through prayer or service.

Chapter 8
Praying "Hard"

Persevere in prayer, with mind awake and thankful heart.
Colossians 4:2 (NEB)

*Greetings from Epaphras, servant of Christ, who is one of yourselves.
He prays hard for you all the time.*
Colossians 4:12 (NEB)

I have difficulty believing some things that I hear in religious circles about prayer. I once saw a book entitled *How to Get What You Want from God through Prayer.* As a local pastor tending to the sick and dying day by day in homes and hospitals, I have often been pained by promises I have heard television or radio preachers make about what God "must do" if we pray. I do not believe that prayer is a device for manipulating God.

I remember Kenny Taylor's funeral. That young father of two small children was a third-generation part of our congregation and as devoted to God and his family as any young man I have ever known.

And then his lungs began to harden unexplainably. As his condition slowly worsened, the prayer intensity of our congregation increased. Finally, a small prayer cell

> *"Praying hard" is holding steadfastly to the faithfulness of God even when the evidence of our longed-for answer is not present. It is submitting to His sovereign design even when it is contrary to our wishes.*

"prayed through" that God was going to heal Kenny. When the word came from Duke University Hospital that Kenny had died, folks from the prayer cell were devastated. His death was sad enough, but the prayer cell members seemed to find it necessary to seek out the person or persons in the congregation whose lack of faith had resulted in Kenny's death. Such a misconception of the nature of God compounded the grief.

I do not believe that God surrenders His sovereignty at our prayer time. And I wouldn't want Him to do so even if He were willing. I see no viable alternative candidate for the role of "Lord of the Universe." I certainly am not qualified for that role.

I like those comments by our Lord when He says, "Do not keep on babbling like the pagans, for they think they will be heard because of their many words. Do not be like them, for your Father knows what you need before you ask him (Matt. 6:7-8 NIV). I repeat: I really do like those passages. They fit the way I think about prayer, and they match the way I like to pray.

But then there are those other stories Jesus tells about the "unjust judge" who finally grants the petition because of persistence (Luke 18). I remember my daddy's preaching dramatically about the man who had company come at midnight only to discover, to his dismay, that his kitchen was out of bread. When his neighbor first refused to get up and give him bread, the man kept knocking on the door until finally—"in order to get a little rest," my daddy would say—the neighbor "got up and threw a whole armload of bread out of the upstairs window" (Luke 11:5-13). (That's what my daddy said. And if he said it was an upstairs window, it must be so.)

Then Dad would encourage us to "keep on knocking." Even as a child, I did not like such thinking. It seemed to make God out to be a cranky neighbor who didn't like being interrupted. In my adulthood, I continued to have some misgivings about "intercessory prayer" and what the implications are for the nature of God.

When Paul says "Persevere in prayer," in Colossians 4:2, he is sounding like my dad, as if we can *finally* get what we want from God *if* we are persistent with Him. I have difficulty with that perception of God.

To make matters worse, Paul soon refers to Epaphras, the one who had told the Colossians about the gospel, and says: "He prays hard for you all the time..." (Col. 4:12).

What does it mean to "pray hard"?

When Barbara and I moved to our first pastorate, our children were small. We had taught them familiar prayers to pray at bedtime. One quiet evening our Debbie, who was just turning four, surprised us. She did not pray as usual: "Dear Jesus, bless Mommy and Daddy and Stevie and me. Give us a good night's rest and a good day tomorrow. Amen!" Instead, she knotted up her tiny fist, began pounding the bedside and calling out as loudly as her little voice could, "Oh, God, help us. Oh, God, help us!" Someone in our new congregation had taught her how to pray "hard." Is that kind of emotional intensity what Paul means?

I am sure that many prayed "hard" for me while I was ill. But what would that mean?

My own engagement with this concept flowered around the years that my mother went through such disorientation with Alzheimer's. I never denied being a "mama's boy." She was at my side to instruct me in my first prayer. And she was there again when, as a seventeen-year-old, I surrendered to God's call upon my life in ministry.

She was there a third time many years later. Our pattern of worship in my last pastorate took me to the people's side of the altar at pastoral prayer time. One Sunday morning as I began to pray, I felt a familiar presence there. Although she was otherwise totally confused, she somehow sensed that her place at prayer time was at the side of her son.

Her deep anxiety was hard for me to take. What an understatement! Let me be more candid. I WAS ANGRY AT GOD. How could He turn my sweet mama, this engaging and gracious hostess of the parsonage, into a half-person, drifting about as an insane person might, all dignity gone and no prospect for improvement? "It isn't fair," I prayed "hard" to God; "I don't claim to be all good, but even I would not do this to her." I was ashamed to pray that way to God, but it was how I felt. Surely that is not what Paul meant by "praying hard."

In the midst of those difficult years, God gave me enriched insights about prayer through my neighbor, a Catholic priest. As fellow pastors, we were participating in a retreat for ministers who served inner-city Nashville. I noticed from the schedule that he was leading our evening devotion and prayer time and silently questioned what he, a Roman Catholic priest, could teach me, a passionate holiness preacher, about prayer. How foolish I was.

In his devotional guidance time, he pointed out that there are three kinds of prayer:

1. Sequential Prayer—This prayer is rational. The one praying may move from a thesis to a conclusion. It is often very much like an essay or term paper. One stays on the subject and presses one's way to a conclusion. In such praying, one may eventually "pray through."

Well, that sounded pretty "right" to me. "Maybe this Catholic brother does know something about prayer after all," I conceded.

He pointed out that most public prayers are of this type. It was natural that we who pray often in public would normally pray in that manner. He smiled as he said, "This kind of prayer is a little difficult for extended prayer times." I thought of times of private devotion when I had "gotten off the subject" with God, when my mind drifted off to a matter that was "not pertinent to my essay." And, of course, there were those times when I had just fallen asleep and awoke with an embarrassed start to apologize to God for straying from the subject.

My brother priest had me with him. He mentioned a second kind of prayer:

> 2. Serendipitous Prayer—The heart of this type of prayer is the fellowship between the one who prays and one's God. YOU DON'T HAVE TO STAY ON THE SUBJECT. With the assurance of His presence, you may wander around all over the prayer landscape to points near or far. If you wander "off of the subject," He will wander there with you to engage in your interest and provide insights concerning it. Even when you nap, you will find Him there when you awake, and He will be pleased that you got some time to rest. Serendipitous prayer has some reason to it, but it is not primarily a rational act. It is joy—even may be fun. It moves with the journey and is often surprising.

"Yeah! That is right!" I almost said it out loud. I thought of times when the work of the church was so consuming that I felt I was talking with the Lord all day long. Often, He seemed to be so real, seated across from me in the car, that I might say out loud, "You really outdid yourself with that sunset! It is beautiful. Thanks!"

And I remembered times when I had advised young mothers, who were feeling guilty that their prayer life was suffering, to "chat with the Lord while you are changing the baby's diaper or doing the dishes. The Lord doesn't mind. He is happy to be there with you."

This second understanding of prayer was making sense to me. He guided me on to a third kind of prayer:

3. Centered Prayer—This kind of prayer is not as rational as sequential prayer is nor does it wander around as serendipitous prayer does. In centered prayer, you ask God for a single insight, word, or characteristic of himself. When He has granted that request, you ask Him to take you into the deep meanings of it. Do not try to make the prayer reasonable. On the other hand, do not let your mind wander as you pray.

I was a bit suspicious. "Is it Christian?" I questioned. But I opened my heart to the Holy Spirit who almost immediately brought to my mind a key Hebrew word from the Old Testament. I am not a Hebrew student, but I know that this word, *kesseth,* means steadfast and unfailing love. It is that awesome characteristic of Jehovah God that was sung by the choirs of Jerusalem in the days of Jehoshaphat when they went out otherwise unarmed, before the armies of the Ammonites and Moabites (II Chron. 20). I would center on this characteristic of God, not by way of essays about His character, nor by way of meandering prayer journeys. I would just focus on *kesseth.*

With this brief but illuminating instruction from my priest friend, to my great amazement two hours had passed with my scarcely knowing it had. As I emerged from that time of prayer, I had no great new rational insight. I still hated the fact that my mother was without a mind. In the ten years that followed before her death, her condition pained me each time I thought about it. However, from that prayer time, I was ever at peace with God. I did affirm that His love is always, really always, faithful. He is true to His word. He loved my mother more than I did, and He did not fail her.

Somewhere along this journey, I think I am beginning to have a sense of what it means to "pray hard." It is

- Job saying, when he could not find God even though he sought him before, behind, to the left, and to the right, "He knows the way that I take and when he has tried me I will come forth as pure gold."

- The captives in Babylon saying, in faith, "Next year Jerusalem" even though they had said it last year and the year before that. They would say it until it was true for them—or for their children.

- Jesus saying in the Garden, "Let this cup pass from me...Nevertheless, not as I will but as thou wilt."

- E. Stanley Jones saying in his last book, *The Divine Yes,* "The darkness may last one day or it may last two, but it never continues through the third day."

"Praying hard" is holding steadfastly to the faithfulness of God even when the evidence of our longed-for answer is not present. It is submitting to His sovereign design even when it is contrary to our wishes. One who "perseveres" in prayer cherishes the continuing relationship with the Father even though the request is not granted at the time or in the way requested. To persevere is to say "Nevertheless," and mean it.

One of my fragmentary memories took place in intensive care and included two of my children, John and Debbie. I learned later that they had been told that they might need to say their "good-byes" to me. I remember saying, "Children, God has been good to your daddy. We have no complaints to make to Him." My memory fades out at that point. They tell me I then asked each of them to pray for me.

In a letter to me Debbie reported the incident like this: "I'll never forget feeling the urgent need to go in and pray for you before leaving for my flight. I asked my Heavenly Father to touch my earthly father and make him whole. I told God that I had been taught by my father to believe in miracles and to ask for them. I asked for a miracle. I literally put my entire life of faith and my father's life into God's loving hands."

I would love to remember her and John's prayers, but I do not. They tell me that they each did pray for my healing. But then they also asked that the Father's will would be done.

Debbie is the same little girl who "prayed hard" back when she was not quite four years of age. I am sure that her voice was subdued when she prayed for me in the intensive care unit. I doubt if she pounded on anything, but I am confident that she had finally, truly learned to "pray hard."

Discoveries on the Way

Prayer is not a device for manipulating God. It is not a mechanism by which I may extend the delusion of my own sovereignty.

In prayer, I submit to His sovereignty and patiently await the unfolding of His patterns for my life to be worked out in His ways.

Enabled by the Holy Spirit, I will declare His lordship in all things and live out that life style through a continuing day-by-day life of prayer.

Chapter 9
Physical and Spiritual Warfare

On that cross he discarded the cosmic powers and authorities like a garment; he made a public spectacle of them and led them as captives in his triumphal procession.

Colossians 2:15 (NEB)

For our fight is not against human foes, but against cosmic powers, against the authorities and potentates of this dark world, against the superhuman forces of evil in the heavens.

Ephesians 6:12 (NEB)

Every power and authority in the universe is subject to him as Head.

Colossians 2:10 (NEB)

"Spiritual warfare" or the interplay of "thrones, sovereignties, authorities, and powers" (Col. 1:16) has always been a little beyond me. I did not focus much on that part of Colossians in my preaching at St. Andrews, nor have I through the years.

I would understand the passages above to say that there are forces of evil present among us but that they have clearly been defeated. The ultimate victory is ours through Jesus Christ.

But the question remains: Do we engage these "powers and authorities" in spiritual battles? He has won the war, but do "skirmishes" or the "minor battles" remain to be fought?

We ARE the "Church militant." We are NOT YET the "Church triumphant." We continue on "the

> *We ARE the "Church militant." We are NOT YET the "Church triumphant." We continue on "the battlefield for our Lord." And sometimes we ARE the battlefield.*

battlefield for our Lord." And sometimes we ARE the battlefield. Satan is sinister enough to take advantage of our every weakness including our physical weakness. We may anticipate that our enemy will be present in every trying situation to seize the opportunity for his advantage.

From the beginning of my illness, I experienced a fierce physical battle. I had been unable to give the doctors any location of pain. As my condition grew worse, I did begin to say, "I feel as if I have warfare going on inside me." I am told that, as my fever raged and my abdomen swelled, I continued to use that expression. My wife, Barbara, tells me that, when she arrived on Wednesday, I said, "Oh, Honey, I have such a terrible battle raging inside of me!"

This kind of "battle" was eventually explained by the doctors who acknowledged that my liver was dying and that nearly three pounds of dead tissue had to be disposed of by my body. Elevated temperature, high enzyme count, the yellowing of my skin, and body-swelling were a few of the signs that an extraordinary physical battle was taking place. No one would doubt that.

But what about a spiritual battle? One would guess that the devil might take advantage of such a time. I have no personal memory of a spiritual battle. But one of my dearest "daughters in the Lord" wrote me of her experience at my side on that first Monday afternoon, and I trust her account.

I mentioned in the previous chapter that Kathy Parker had dropped by on Monday. Kathy's grandparents, Alonzo and Corinne Gentry, were long-time members of my church in Nashville and some of my "dearest." Both were retired when we moved to Nashville, but Brother Gentry was still painting, and he repainted the parsonage as we were moving in. We had hours of great fellowship while he painted and I "helped."

Stan and Kathy found each other in our college-age Sunday school class and soon romance blossomed toward marriage. I had mixed feelings when they went off to seminary. I knew they would make fine pastors, but I would miss them, especially Kathy's beautiful soprano voice at solo time.

My prediction had come true. They pastored well in South Carolina right there in Charleston. Their first son was a student at Trevecca at that time, so our ties were especially close.

I had hoped that we might get together on Saturday of my weekend in Charleston, but I had felt so bad that I delayed—sending word through Pastor Fountain that I would like for them to come see me in the hospital. Kathy and her teenage son, Ryan, came by on Monday. Here is part of Kathy's report of their visit.

"When we arrived at the hospital and walked inside, I knew I'd like to get a card, so we went to the gift shop where we could not find even one 'religious' card. Hence, the silly 'hospital humor.'

At this time, neither of us had any inkling as to how seriously ill you really were.

"We walked into your hallway, found your name on the doorjamb, and, at that moment, before I looked any further, I knew something was terribly wrong. I have never even discussed this with Stan, but there was a very definite feeling in the air around me. As we stepped off the elevator, I sensed something in the air, a stirring, something I cannot put into words which will accurately describe it, a tension-like fog or mist even though the hallway was very brightly lighted.

"As Ryan and I walked toward your door, this feeling became stronger with each step. I knew something was going on inside. I ignored it and looked through the door to see you talking on the phone—talking ever so gently and coherently with Melvin at your side.

"When you saw me, you said out loud, 'Oh, I see the face of an angel!' and I knew it was okay for me to have come. (I guess I had been a little afraid that you would have been, perhaps, embarrassed for me to be in your room.)

"I was overwhelmed by being called an 'angel' but still sensed this awful 'presence' which I could not explain but which was very, very oppressive.

"You said good-bye into the phone, and Melvin reached to take it from you since we had eased into the room near your bedside.

"Again, you said to me, 'I am so glad to see your face. No one has ever looked so like an angel to me.' And then you took my hand in yours, and I bent down and kissed your beard-roughened cheek.

"Millard, please forgive me when I tell you that I am crying as I write this, but I wanted to cry then. Your skin was so very hot and dry to the touch. Your always-groomed appearance was one of flyaway hair and mismatched hospital attire. You had name bands where your watch should have been. Your skin was an ashen hue of yellow but very pink too. Where you had always had conscious control of your movements, you seemed to be surprised by seeing your hand move or your foot settling in the covers. You seemed worn and helpless in your illness.

"With some effort, we carried on a conversation about our mutual interests. The whole time we talked, I held your hand and you gripped mine. It was as if you *needed* to touch someone. I don't know for sure, but I know I needed to touch you because a presence/tension/air of hate and anger was *right over my head, right over your bed!* I wish this did not sound so weird, but I can't explain it any other way. I kept trying to ignore it, hoping it would go away, needing, wanting it to disperse. It didn't.

"A nurse came in at one point and I started to leave, but she said, 'No, no, you may stay. I am just checking numbers.' I had pulled away from you then, but as I turned back, you took my hand again and said, 'Kathy, will you please pray for me?'

"Immediately, a thousand things occurred at once. You closed your eyes and turned your face up to God. I thought to myself, What? Me? Pray for Millard Reed? A man who has prayed some of the most beautiful prayers I have ever heard? What do I say for this holy man?

"All the noises from the hallway became magnified and amplified. Melvin touched your leg through the sheets of the bed where you lay. Ryan cleared his throat, closed his eyes, and shifted his weight from one foot to the other. AND THE AIR ABOVE US BECAME ALIVE—I can find no other descriptive word—with feelings of death and anger and vileness and hate. The picture now in my mind is of clouds rolling overhead, but there were no actual clouds in the room, only a very real and terrible feeling.

"I never closed my eyes as I prayed for you, Millard. To be perfectly honest, I believe I was afraid to close them, afraid of what my mind would see around us.

"So I prayed.

"I wanted to scream, to shout, to yell at whatever was with us, to demand that it leave us alone.

"I believe I would have been justified in doing so. I wish I had, but I also know that I was scared. Scared of whatever was happening over our heads. Scared of what was happening in your body. Scared of praying the wrong thing. Scared.

"I put some phrases together and said, 'Amen.' You squeezed my hand and told me thanks for my sweet prayer. I still don't remember what I said.

"I bent and kissed your cheek a second time and turned to leave.

"Please believe me, Millard, when I say that there was an unreal, spiritual battle going on concerning you. You *have* been kept on earth for a reason. You *have* been divinely healed. You are alive because God willed it so.

"I was scared, confused, and knew my own inadequacies while with you, but I *never* felt hopeless or lost or uncertain of your healing. The oppression in your room was only the posturing of

Satan. A real and earnest battle? Yes, but one whose outcome was predetermined from its very inception. God's sweet presence assured me of that as I stood in your room. I feel a bit of a coward for not having shared this with anyone until now, but I have not experienced too many of these and do not have much confidence in myself. Forgive me.

"Needless to say, I was not too surprised when we heard that God was making you a new liver.

"To you, I may have had the face of an angel, but God's angels were already in your room before I ever arrived."

When Barbara read Kathy's letter, she said, "I praise God for sending Kathy to your side. I praise Him for giving her the spiritual insight not only to feel *His presence* but also to recognize and feel the presence of Satan, who definitely was working hard to win the battle—to try to cause all of us to lose faith in our Lord and Savior Jesus Christ! The devil knew your work, Millard, and was working overtime to end it."

My memories of Kathy's visit are very limited. I do remember her face shining with an angelic glow. I do believe that Satan does all he can to intimidate and defeat us in our times of trial and sickness. And I do believe that the ONE that is in us is GREATER than the one that is in the world.

Discoveries on the Way

I am no match for the enemy of my soul. But I do not depend on my own spiritual energy for the battle. "Every power and authority in the universe" (Col. 2:10) is available to me through Christ.

Satan is already a defeated foe. The skirmishes that we are engaged in are fearsome all right, but our deliverance is assured and our victory is a certainty.

I will "fight the good fight," but I will not do it in my own energy. The battle is the Lord's. I am His foot soldier.

Chapter 10
Prayer with Anointing

Is anyone among you sick? Let him call for the elders of the church, and let them pray over him, anointing him with oil in the name of the Lord. And the prayer of faith will save the sick, and the Lord will raise him up.

James 5:14 (NKJV)

On that cross he discarded the cosmic powers and authorities like a garment; he made a public spectacle of them and led them as captives in his triumphal procession.

Colossians 2:15 (NEB)

While many prayers were ascending to the Father on my behalf, from many places, I had not yet been anointed with oil as the Scripture instructs. That ancient biblical rite took place back in Nashville at the hands of my own pastors. I will share with you how I got back to Nashville in the next section. For now, I want to share a further word on prayer and anointing. It is another portion of the story of which I have no memory. I depend on my pastor, Dr. Gary Allen Henecke, to tell it:

Can you believe that He holds "all things" together?

"We received news of the sudden illness of [President Reed] on Monday following his hospitalization. The first reports were not taken seriously because they were stated so bleakly, and I know that in Christian circles the rumor mill often exaggerates the prayer needs. Yet, for me, the pastor of the First Church of the Nazarene in Nashville, Tennessee, an illness that requires the hospitalization of the president of Trevecca has special significance. Since we are 'the Mother Church' of the University, we have a responsibility to Dr. and Mrs. Reed and a connection between our peoples that goes way beyond laity and employees. Dr. Reed is not only a part of this congregation, but he has been pastor of this church for the second-longest tenure of its hundred-year history. He is held in high esteem and affection by those who had the privilege of being pastored by him. And he has been a personal brother to me. I have been his booster. My friend was ill.

"The initial phone call gave the reports of 'life-threatening' conditions. No one wanted to use those words in the initial moments, but the seriousness of the situation continued to grow. By Wednesday evening, we reviewed the seriousness of his condition with the Board, even including discussion about what would be the Church's role in supporting the University should a funeral occur.

"The news of the decision to fly Dr. Reed to Nashville arrived in the church office on Friday. I was now enough a part of the conversation with the University leadership and the local church that I knew the success of such a journey was questionable. Immediately, the prayer chains of First Church were activated—from prayers for an available liver for transplant to prayers for their former pastor's safety in flight.

"When the actual flight was announced and begun from South Carolina, we were made aware of as much detail as was available through telephone conversations with the family there. After verifying the exact time of landing with the local ambulance flight service, I made contact with my assistant pastor, Rev. Michael Benson, and asked him if he would accompany me to the hospital where we might have a moment with the family and, if possible, a time to pray personally for and anoint the president.

"Prayers for healing have been a vital part of my ministry, and my faith in the ancient ritual of the church is ever deepening. The unction of the oil, accompanied by faith, has been central to my concept of the ministry of the church. It was not unusual or mysterious that we waited in the intensive care unit with a bottle of oil in our hands. It was, rather, after our pattern.

"Soon after the sound of sirens and the flash of lights brought him into the driveway of the Vanderbilt emergency room, I was in conversation with Barbara. Not long after that, Mike and I were allowed to enter the intensive care room to which he had been assigned. We assured him of the prayers and concerns of those who loved him in his hometown. The prayer of faith was a simple prayer spoken with only a few sentences. As is my custom, I used the oil to form a cross on my brother's forehead and prayed for divine healing in the name of Jesus. There was no prayer for a liver or for a surgery. There was prayer for the wisdom of the doctors and the miracle of God. The rest is now history."

Would you now re-read the Scriptures from James and Colossians printed at the top of this chapter? James gives the command, and Paul gives the rationale for the prayer for healing. The crucial question behind the prayer for divine healing is CAN YOU, AS A TWENTIETH-CENTURY PERSON, BELIEVE COLOSSIANS 2:15? Can you believe that Jesus of Nazareth holds the power of all creation (Col. 1:15-20)? The philosophers would ask, "Can you accept a first-century cosmology?"

Bear in mind that when John the Beloved turns to the task of telling the Jesus story he must re-tell the creation story. In John, chapter one, he does a very extraordinary thing. He begins to recite Genesis 1:1, "In the beginning. . . ." That phrase was very familiar. Every Hebrew child knew it by heart. It is the beginning of the creation story. But then John does what every Hebrew child would consider blasphemy. He alters the script! He changes the words. One must never, never do that. But John does it. He must do it. For he has taken on the task of introducing his readers to the One who activated the creation. The "Word," the One by whom the universe came into existence, who was from the beginning, "came to dwell among us" as the "Father's only Son" (1:14). Jesus, about whom John wants to give the full story, is the one who created the worlds and all that are in them. Radical cosmology!

But long before John wrote his gospel, Paul is making this radical declaration in his letter to the Colossians: "ALL THINGS ARE HELD TOGETHER IN HIM" (Col. 1:17).

And the question to the twentieth-century pagan is "Can you believe that?"

Can you, with your enlarged knowledge of the universe, with interplanetary rocketships and the "big bang" and "dark holes," believe that Jesus of Nazareth, who was born of a young maiden in an obscure village in a subservient country, who never traveled more than a few miles from His home town, and who was disgraced in His death—CAN YOU BELIEVE THAT HE HOLDS "ALL THINGS" TOGETHER?

That is what one must believe in order to pray the prayer of faith for the sick because the miniature "universe" of disease and germs is more profound than the immense "universe" of space. And if one is to pray the prayer of faith for healing one must believe that He holds it all together and sets it in order by His will.

That is what one must believe if one is to pray for healing. More importantly, it is what one must believe in order to be Christian.

That is "who" Jesus is by the New Testament faith. Not just a great teacher. Not just a kindly healer of the sick. Not just a benevolent giver to the poor. He is the center of the universe. HE HOLDS IT ALL TOGETHER.

Now, if one believes that, one has little, if any, trouble obeying the instruction of Scripture, picking up a vial of oil, and anointing the sick for healing. The One who holds it all together—whose mind created and maintains the molecular consistency of the oil, who created the hand that administers it, who made possible the voice that prays and created the body anointed—is able to do as He wills in response to His beloved.

I do not remember being anointed. The smudge of oil was long since gone from my forehead by the time I revived. But I am deeply grateful to my pastors for obeying the word of Scripture and for ministering to me in my time of need. I have done it many times for others before and since that time. The God who was and is will be faithful until He comes.

<hr />

Discoveries on the Way

The rituals of the Church are established by God himself. He who made himself known in human flesh by the incarnation of His son has also chosen to establish earthly patterns of worship which He is pleased to honor by His presence.

He promises always to be present in the waters of baptism and the elements of the Lord's Supper.

He has also instructed that the sick be anointed with oil and prayed for by the elders. It is His pattern.

I will look forward to and enter into every design for rendezvous that God lays out for me. He makes the appointments. I am happy to meet Him in them.

Chapter 11
Children in the "Christian Way"

Children, obey your parents in everything, for that is pleasing to God and is the Christian way.

Colossians 3:20 (NEB)

I think I am a typical "daddy" in that I always want to be there for my family in their times of crisis.

Our family has been very fortunate in that we have had no major crises and very few that were even minor. This sickness of mine has been our most dramatic moment—AND I WASN'T THERE! The one aspect of this whole episode that fills me with regret is the fact that I was not with my family in their time of great anxiety. I know that such a concern is foolish. I WAS there! I was the cause for their anxiety. But I have no memory of being there for them, and while my mind knows better, my emotions feel guilty for not being there for them when they needed me.

> *My family exhibited great strength of character, and what makes it worse, (please indulge my foolishness) they did it without me. How dare they?!*

That week, enclosed by the last Sunday of February and the first Sunday of March, has almost no place in my memory. I can recall only scattered seconds that might total a minute or two. But those eight days are the vivid memory of a lifetime for my family. And I was in intensive care and not at their sides. I still feel bad about my "absence."

My first call to Barbara on the February Sunday evening was misleading. My misrepresentation of the situation was not intentional on my part. I had just always been so well that I was confident that I would be out of the hospital and on my way in a few hours. I suggested that she not trouble the children or notify the College. I promised her that I would call back the next morning.

By Monday, midday, I was quickly losing my mental powers so that when she called I couldn't make sense to her or myself, and I asked Melvin to take the phone. From that point, anxiety levels began to skyrocket in the Reed household.

Without Barbara's knowledge, the school had learned of my hospitalization so that when our daughter, Debbie, called to talk to me at my office Monday morning, she was informed that I was in the hospital. That information prompted a quick call from Debbie to her mother, then to her brothers, and then to my brothers and sister. The word was still one of guarded optimism: "He really is sick but will probably be okay."

The Reed family has always tended to be pretty low key. However, when they heard the Monday afternoon diagnosis of "liver failure" with "the likely need of a liver transplant," their calm demeanor became a deep, deep anxiety as they gradually began to deal with the possibility that they would likely lose their husband, father, and brother.

How does a family respond at such times? How would MY FAMILY respond? I suppose that I have always felt that there is a deep strength in our family that would handle such a time with grace, but one doesn't know until the time comes. There is no way to practice for such a time or go through rehearsals. The time arrives, and when it does, it proves the character and strength of a family. My family exhibited great strength of character, and what makes it worse, (please indulge my foolishness) they did it without me. How dare they?!

🙐🙐🙐 🙐🙐🙐 🙐🙐🙐

Two events made the unbelievable become more and more obvious to Barbara and the children: I was transferred to the University of South Carolina Medical Center on Tuesday, and my doctors informed Barbara that "a transplant must be done within a few days."

My family began to rethink the situation and reasoned, "Dad could be dying. We must rush there if we want to see him. What should we do? Charleston is an eight- to ten-hour drive from Nashville. Flight connections are difficult through Atlanta. John [the youngest sibling] is in Chicago. What about Aunt Martha [my sister]? She is recording in Quincy, Illinois, with Uncle Marvin. Should they come? Uncle Harold is not able to travel. And Mom is still having serious trouble with her back since surgery. The long drive would be especially painful. What would Dad want us to do? What would he tell us if he could?"

By one means or another, Barbara and the children were in Charleston by early Thursday morning. Debbie and Barbara had flown on Delta the night before. Sons Stephen and Paul had driven by way of Atlanta, and John had flown from Chicago. Aunt Martha, Uncle Marvin, Uncle Harold, and Aunt Dorothy would keep in touch by phone and hold us in their prayers. After a thorough briefing from the team of doctors who reviewed how serious my situation was, my family was allowed to enter my intensive care room.

What followed was one of my ten-second memories. I remember their surrounding me with a mood of deep, loving concern. Their arrival climaxed a terrible three days. Phone calls with bad news. Arrangements to make. Flights to schedule and catch. Long miles to cover on the highway. Now, at long last, they had made it to my side. They were smitten by how bad I looked. My skin was a bronzed yellow color. I had four days of beard because my blood-clotting factors were so low that they dared not shave me. They questioned, "Is he conscious? Will he be able to speak to us?"

As they gathered around me, I sensed that they were eager to hear some word, maybe a final parting word, from their father. I felt I must respond. I summoned every bit of energy I had. I cleared my voice as best as I could. It was little more than a breathy wheeze. "Be sure to take in the tourist attractions while you are here in Charleston," I said. Can you imagine my suggesting something so foolish?

As the "wise head of the clan," I provided what could have been my last words on earth to my precious family, and I gave them a "Chamber of Commerce commercial" for Charleston.

I remember their looking at me as if I had lost my mind. I guess I had. It was too somber a situation for laughter but too silly to take seriously. I remember being amused at what had come out of my own mouth and sensed that they were amused too. I then faded into unconsciousness and have no further memory of their being in Charleston.

Since that week of crisis, all of the children have commented on how they seemed to slip back into their childhood sibling roles. Even though their ages now range from thirty-three to forty-two, the dynamic of their relationships seemed to be dictated by the way that they related as siblings when they were around the kitchen table.

Stephen was once again the "big brother." Maybe it is that role from childhood that has equipped him to become vice president for financial planning with First American Bank in Nashville.

In Charleston, he led the conversations with the doctors, made sure that Mom was cared for, and received inquiry from the school and the church. Since he was a qualified financial planner, I had kept him informed regarding my plans for retirement as well as my death. Now he was facing it not as a remote possibility but as an imminent likelihood.

Just ten days earlier I had made the first premium payment on an insurance policy that would create a sizable endowment for scholarships at Trevecca. He had handled the transaction and was one of the few persons who was aware of it. The policy would have been a tremendous return for the school but one that he earnestly hoped would not develop.

He could not avoid the "what if" questions and was running ahead in his mind to seek for the preferred answer. What if there is no liver available? Should we get him back to Nashville? Would he survive the flight? What if he dies here? Is the will in place? Can Mom live alone?

During all the heavy conversations with the doctors that laced both Thursday and Friday, Stephen was feeling the load of leadership. A family cannot create this atmosphere artificially. The anxiety was not hypothetical. It was real. The "older brother" was feeling the concern of the family—a concern that was painfully real.

Debbie was my advocate.

From the time she was two years old, Debbie always seemed to take responsibility for everyone. She was always "a little mother." She would call her brother "**my** Stephen" in those days. Of course, that attitude often meant she expected folks to be accountable to her. I used to call her "my little straw boss."

We have not been surprised to see her choose education as a career and special education as her ministry. Day-by-day in the classroom, she cares for some twelve handicapped children who are "her" children.

In my curiosity to learn what had been going on during the time I was unconscious, I asked the children to write me notes. Here is a part of Debbie's notes:

"When my brothers arrived, we each took our roles and began to ride an emotional roller coaster. We became students of medicine, learning what was critical to watch for. The doctors brought us sobering information about liver transplants. They explained the small percentage of success. But they said that IF a donor liver was ready and IF the transplant went well and IF the blood-clotting factor was high enough (it was NOT high enough just now) that Dad might be all right. So how do we pray? Make someone else die so Dad can live? No, I did not like that idea. I decided to pray for a miracle.

"Later that evening, we waited for more than forty-five minutes past our time to see Dad AND THEY WOULD NOT LET US IN. Mother cooperated and accepted their poor excuses for not allowing us to go in. I, on the other hand, bit my tongue and left very annoyed that I was not allowed to say good night to my dad. After we returned to our motel rooms, the hospital called to tell us that Dad was much worse. Needless to say, I had a few words with the head nurse about the way they needed to work on their compassion and manners when dealing with the families in the critical care unit. We did not sleep that night."

Later Debbie learned why the family had been kept away from me. The nurses told Debbie that they could not allow my family into the unit that night because a patient in that same intensive care unit had died that evening. A young thirty-three-year-old man who also had hepatitis had died, and the nurses were serving the young man's family that night.

During the extended time in intensive care, both in Charleston and in Nashville, my little girl was nearly always at my side, taking care of "her daddy."

Paul, our third child, was always the communicator both in word and song.

When Stephen and Debbie were in grade school, they entered a singing contest sponsored by the church. At the last minute Paul, who was not quite five years old, asked to enter, and so we let him. He sang a song he already knew by heart: "I am so glad that Jesus loves me. Jesus loves me. Jesus loves me. I am so glad that Jesus loves me. Jesus loves even me!" The "cute little boy" charmed the judges and won the contest, much to the dismay of his older brother and sister.

Paul is still enjoying success. Today it is in sales with a computer firm that provides bar code scanners for a variety of applications. He sings in the local opera from time to time, and he and his wife, Lisa, are faithful in the choir at Nashville's First Church of the Nazarene.

Because of the great flood of telephone calls coming into the hospital, the administrators provided a special suite with phone and refreshments for our family and visitors to use. Much of the time, Paul was there to receive calls and answer questions as best he could. He was still in communications.

John Mark, our youngest, was always our artist—but not simply an artist who can see and make a picture. He is that kind of artist—but he also has the ability to sense how another feels.

Even when he was very small, he was "gifted" with the ability to know when I needed a hug. Many times such a hug provided a "little boy tonic" for some grown-up stress I was bearing.

John never seemed to hear the call of the Lord upon his life. Maybe his sensitivity to the feelings of his peers drowned out God's voice and made their influence on him so harmful during his teen years. I never doubted John's love for me, and I think he was confident of my love for him, but I often felt him absent from "our Father's house" and yearned to see him "home" during the years of his searching.

Various eclectic or New Age "faiths" held some fascination for him along the way. We would talk about them from time to time. During premarital counseling when he and Angie were married, some six years ago, I asked John about his faith. He thought a long time and finally said, "I think" (he paused a moment for further refection), "I think I believe in love."

"And so do I," I responded. "We are in agreement on that. But I have also sensed a need to be more specific in how love is expressed. I have found the specific expression of the love of God in Jesus Christ through His teachings, death, and resurrection. The day may come when you will also want to be more specific in how love is expressed toward you. When that day comes, I hope you will accept it as I have accepted it in Jesus Christ."

Through these years, I can see such acceptance happening in John. When he got the word of my illness, he was doing post-bac work in art at the Chicago Art Institute. By the time the family made contact with him, the message was pretty grim. John was alone. His dad needed a hug and he was not there to give it. In a burst of emotion, he ran out of his loft apartment onto the streets of Chicago, looking for a church in which to pray. In time, he found a Catholic church and was relieved to find it open. Kneeling inside an ornate sanctuary he prayed, "Oh, Jesus, don't let my daddy die!" He had come to a time of need and was happy to be specific in his prayer.

His "little brother" role in the family was less defined. His heart was heavy, and he didn't mind that his concern showed. He was not interested in conversations with the doctors about charts and numbers. He just wanted them to heal his dad. Doctors are supposed to heal sick people. Dad is sick. If these doctors cannot heal him, let's find some who can. "Big brothers'" explanations about the limits that doctors had were of no comfort.

🙐   🙐   🙐

While preaching from Colossians in Charleston, I had not focused on chapter three, verse twenty, but I thought of it often during my convalescence: "Children, obey your parents in everything, for that is pleasing to God and is the Christian way."

The word "obey" seems a bit inappropriate in our case since neither Barbara nor I was giving them orders. Quite to the contrary. I was fully dependent and Barbara needed their wisdom and help. But they did honor us by the way they conducted themselves, and their doing so gave us a deep assurance that our years of earnest prayer and effort to be good parents in "God's way" had not been in vain.

Their "obedience" during our family crisis brought great pride to Barbara and me. It reminded us of one of our favorite two-part family stories.

Part I. When their age range was four through thirteen, they all took piano lessons. After some months of hard work it was time for the recital which was held in the formal atmosphere of the seminary. Their teacher, Miss Kathy, started with her smallest students, and after each thirty-second performance there was a very polite staccato of applause.

After about three or four such performances had been completed, it was time for John, the first entry from the Reed clan. As he performed, the remaining five of us, each of whom had heard the simple melody line at least a hundred times, were leaning forward in our seats, pulling for John's each and every note. And he completed the song without an error! Everyone else applauded politely as we had done for the others. But Paul, who was just three years older than John, could not contain his pride and joy. "WAY TO BE, JOHN!" he yelled at the top of his seven-year-old voice.

Well, that incident remained an inside family joke for us through the years. When anyone of our family performed especially well in some effort, we would say, "Way to be, John—or Paul—or Debbie—or Steve." That chant of approval was one of those family trademarks that every family creates through the years of shared living.

Part II. The story has another chapter that took place nearly thirty years later. I mentioned that Paul would sometimes sing in chorus with the local opera. Barbara and I would routinely take in his performance at the Tennessee Performance Arts Center in Nashville.

On one occasion, we arrived early to find our seats and look over the program. We found—to our surprise—that our son had a solo part. It was a very small part that the traveling opera company apparently gave to some local performer. They had chosen him.

You can imagine our pride as Paul had his moment of "stardom." He got through the tiny part well, and we were pleased.

Then the opera was over and it was time for the curtain call. We expected him to take his bow with the chorus as in the past. But suddenly it dawned on me; "He did a solo! He will have a personal bow." It just happened that Barbara and I were on the front row of the first balcony, dead center. And now my son was beginning his bow. Should I do it? If I am going to do it, I must do it now, and I must do it as loudly as I can if he is going to hear me.

"WAY TO BE, PAUL!" I yelled as loudly as I possibly could. He was deep in his bow, and when he heard my voice, he bolted upright to full height.

Barbara was so embarrassed. Everyone around us was smiling. I was as happy as a clown. I was able to repeat a family liturgy to my son at a dramatic moment.

And Paul was happy too. When we got down to the stage floor, he told us that other actors were commenting about his "private fan club." Soon, our oldest son, Stephen, who was in the back of the balcony, came toward us saying, "I knew you would do that!"

I tell this family story because it expresses how proud I am of them. I believe their care for me pleased God. It is "the Christian way."

But it is also so very assuring to each of us that the character of our family, a character that has been forged through years of value- and priority-setting, proved to be strong in the time of crisis.

"WAY TO BE, STEPHEN, DEBBIE, PAUL, AND JOHN!"

Discoveries on the Way

The family is the design of the Lord, and the privilege of being a parent is one of life's great responsibilities. It is also great fun. The love ties of human families are His sweet gifts.

I will carry out this sacred responsibility, not as a duty but as a pleasure, and trust that my children will see something of the Heavenly Father in the life of their earthly father.

Chapter 12
Barbara, My Partner

Wives, understand and support your husbands by submitting to them in ways that honor the Master. Husbands, go all out in love for your wives. Don't take advantage of them.

Colossians 3:18-19 (*The Message*)

My illness enriched my relationship with Barbara, my wife of forty-three years. We have always been "partners," but the unfolding drama in Charleston caused that partnership to be strengthened in several ways. I probably would have denied it in my youth, but from the perspective I now hold, I THINK I HAVE LOVED BARBARA ALL MY LIFE.

> *Through all of these experiences, we have been partners— singing partners, prayer partners, and marriage partners.*

My first sight of her is still very vivid in my mind. The kids from Tilden Grade School, where she attended, came to Eugene Field for their ninth year. She walked into Miss Troutman's homeroom class, and I was smitten.

Before the year was out, we began singing together. Our first duet was a part of the ninth-grade spring musical: "Sweetheart, Sweetheart, Sweetheart, Will you love me ever? Will you remember the day When we were happy in May, My dearest one?"

We have pretty much made music together since that time. We dated as juniors and seniors in high school and sang in the choirs and ensembles at school.

Soon after our graduation from high school, I went off to youth camp where I was wonderfully saved and acknowledged my call to preach. Upon returning home, I told my girl friend of this life-changing experience and suggested that our dating relationship should end. She didn't follow my logic.

Within a few weeks, my preacher dad was hospitalized for a minor ailment. The people of the church who had recently heard me witness to a call to preach said, "Well, Millard, you are called to preach. You bring the message next Sunday morning!"

I agreed and informed my Presbyterian girl friend that I would be preaching on Sunday morning and that IF she wanted to come it would be okay. (Very mild evangelism. I didn't even offer to provide a ride for her.)

My message was simple but heartfelt. I drew on the story of Jesus' calming the waves and raised the rhetorical question of Matthew 8:27, "What manner of man is this, that even the winds and the waves obey him!" My sermon was mostly a testimony of what Jesus had so recently become to me. I opened the altar for seekers but no one came, and so I prayed a closing prayer and went to the side room just off the platform.

Meanwhile, God was talking to Barbara. Her church background did not include a public invitation. She has always said that her heart was pounding so loudly that she thought all the folks in the sanctuary must have been hearing it. She had tried to move past her mother toward the altar at the invitation time, but her mother had assured her that she [Barbara] was fine and did not need to go to the altar.

A precious woman in the service sensed that the Holy Spirit was speaking to Barbara, went to her side as the service was dismissed, and asked if she would like to pray. That encouragement was all Barbara needed. Soon a teenage girl, who had been hungry for the Lord all her life, was kneeling at the altar and pouring out her heart to "the one who calmed the winds and the waves."

My brother Harold found me in the side room and informed me that my girl friend had come to the altar. I suspect that I am one of a very few preachers who married his first convert.

Through college, seminary, pastorates, graduate work, and now as we serve the University, we have been partners. She has directed Bible schools, planned Christmas plays, led children's church, and hosted board parties. (I started to say "social events," but Barbara's activities were more than "social events"; they were "PARTIES.")

A thousand or so pizzas and nearly that many decorated cakes and hot fudge sundaes and taco meals were all a part of her entertainment "specialties." Along the way, several children stayed in our home, including the children of missionaries. Some stayed for as long as nine months.

And all the time we accepted every opportunity to sing together. At youth gatherings it was "Sipping Cider through a Straw." Sunday nights it might be "Old-Fashioned Meeting in an Old-Fashioned Place." Sunday morning it would sometimes be "Wonderful, Wonderful Jesus" or "My Heart Is Stirred Whene'er I Think of Jesus." Sometimes in a nursing home or a hospital death room it would be "Christ Is Not a Disappointment." When the children were small, we might have to send "looks of discipline" while we were singing. Once while trying to sing in Spanish for a congregation in Central America, we ran out of words before we ran out of melody line. Our listeners smiled and seemed to appreciate our effort.

Through all of these experiences, we have been partners— singing partners, prayer partners, and marriage partners.

Maybe my desire to protect her is part of the reason why I did not want to alarm her when I first called from Charleston. She says that when she and the children arrived the first thing I said was, "Oh, Honey, I am so sorry that you have had to come all this distance."

Once they had seen me and heard the dark predictions of the doctor, Barbara could not sleep. After they were not allowed to see me on that Thursday night, my wife, who showed absolutely no signs of nausea through four pregnancies, was desperately ill through the night with repeated dry heaves.

The great debate on Friday was whether I could survive a flight back to Nashville. Barbara wanted me "home." She felt—accurately, I think—that even though I was unconscious, I sensed that it would be better for me back in Nashville for surgery, for recovery, or even for death.

But doctors were opposed to the idea—"especially the lady doctor with the South American accent." Barbara told me later, "This lady doctor kept repeating to me over and over again, 'This is the best place for a transplant. We have the highest percentage of successful liver transplants in the country. More livers are available in South Carolina. If you put him on that plane, he will go into a coma and he will die before you get to Nashville.' And dear Dr. Rashford, although he was no longer officially your physician, pleaded with us to stay in South Carolina, suggesting that our family could live with them in their home. Even the children were inclined to agree. And Uncle Marvin called to suggest, 'Better alive in South Carolina than dead in Nashville.' "

"But I knew," Barbara has told me, "that you would not be comfortable until you were back home. So I told the doctors, 'You have not told me anything new. You tell me that if he doesn't get a liver here he will die. And if he doesn't get a liver in Nashville he will die. And by your own admission, his blood count is so low just now that you couldn't do surgery even if you had a liver. His situation is as hopeless in one place as it is in the other. He wants to go back to Nashville, so that settles it. We will go back to Nashville.'" (I asked her later who decided to bring me back to Nashville. She said that I did. Again, I have no memory. And I suspect that her conclusion may have been based on her reading of me, a reading which I do not doubt was anything other than accurate. We still harmonize pretty well.)

With the decision made to fly me back to Nashville in an ambulance plane, the family scattered "like water on a hot skillet." Steve and Paul would drive in cavalcade with Melvin. Debbie and John would take a commercial flight. And Barbara? What about Barbara? Would there be room on the tiny ambulance craft? Could she endure a flight in a small plane with her recent back problems?

Soon the flight officials indicated that two pilots would fly the plane, two medical personnel would attend to me, and a seat alongside my gurney would accommodate her. Here we go—one more adventure for Barbara and Millard.

She tells me that I was very restless, that my greatly distended abdomen made the restrictions extremely difficult for me. I kept whispering to her in such a way that the other attendants would not hear, "Let's get out of here." Again and again, "Let's get out of here." Along in the flight, when I noticed the door, I said, "There's the door, let's you and I slip out." "Well, okay, if you insist," she finally said. "We have done a lot of things together. We could go out that door, but the first step is a very long one." As the Bonanza ambulance plane droned on toward Nashville, she found herself singing, partially for me and partially for herself, the song that had held her steady as a new Christian. Over and over the refrain found itself in her mind and voice: "Many things about tomorrow, I don't seem to understand. But I know who holds tomorrow, And I know who holds my hand."

"Throughout the flight," Barbara told me later, "I did not think of coma once. I KNEW that God was in control of our situation."

The only thing I recall about the flight was a single phrase from her. I remember her acting like a stewardess and saying, "Coffee, tea, or me? On our flights we like to keep our passengers comfortable." And I remember the attendants' laughing at her.

Contrary to the predictions of the lady doctor from South America, I took the trip very well. Barbara was frightened only once when my attention drifted away from the door and I said that I could see a very bright moon. Barbara could see no moon and feared that I might be seeing the "white light" that many see in the hour of death. When the plane landed in Nashville and she emerged through "the door," she saw a very bright moon. From my angle on the gurney, I had seen what she could not see.

The two-and-one-half-hour flight from Charleston, through some rain and turbulence, brought us to Nashville at about nine-thirty. Soon the ambulance had me in place, and Barbara was at the side of the driver watching him activate the computer that sent lights flashing and warning signals sounding as we raced at high speed toward Vanderbilt Hospital.

Pastors Henecke and Benson, Dean Steve Pusey and his wife (Gail), daughter-in-law Lisa and her parents (the Tates), and Joyce Welch were awaiting our arrival at the emergency room. Soon the boys called on their mobile phone as they drove through Atlanta, "Did he make it? Is Mom okay?" Good news: "Both are doing well."

It was well after midnight by the time I had been processed and placed in intensive care and after I had been anointed and prayed for by the pastors. It was almost 4:00 a.m. when the boys and Melvin arrived to take my "partner" home for a little bit of rest. It had been an unbelievable day for her. She had engaged in the long discussion about the flight. She had taken the risk to fly me to Nashville, a risk that others, even the family, might not have forgiven her for if I had died in flight. She had expended awesome energy attending to me during the turbulent flight. But now the traumatic day was done. "The doctors in Nashville have had no better word than the doctors in Charleston had," she thought to herself, "but at least he is home. If he dies, he will die at home."

As she put a few of my clothes in the familiar dresser, in the familiar bedroom, in our familiar home, she thought, "Well, Barbara, your mother was a widow at age sixty-three. History may be repeating itself. You and Millard may never get to sing together again."

During the next few days, she assumed the role of "hostess" at the hospital as so many friends and folks whom we had pastored from the Nashville area came by to share and pray. She often provided consolation for them by assuring them that they should not worry because God was in control.

During the weeks of my convalescence, she was my "beloved warden" making sure that I did not take phone calls or otherwise overdo. When I felt very weak, she was there to encourage me.

After a few weeks, maybe it was three months, we were asked if we would like to sing together for the Regional Senior Adult Conference. Would we like to sing together? Just give us a chance! We selected a song that would not be too difficult for me. How precious the experience was as we sang for the first time in months: "Surely goodness and mercy shall follow me all the days, all the days of my life. When I walk through that dark lonesome valley, my Savior will walk with me there."

Old song. New, rich meaning!

Throughout my adult life, I have enjoyed two great "constants." Two things that are just "givens." They are not debated in my mind. They are simply true. They are (1) my call to preach—God must have known that I could not doubt His call and serve as He wanted me to—and (2) my love for Barbara. He brought us together and He has given us a song that has been a joy to share.

Barbara's service in love reminds me of Paul's brief statement in Colossians 1:24. There he gives testimony concerning his love for the Colossians. "It is now my happiness to suffer for you," he writes. "It is my way of helping to complete in my human flesh the full tale of Christ's affliction still to be endured, for the sake of his body which is the church."

In the Western World we are inclined to think of suffering as private. It is a thing to be dealt with by a "stiff upper lip" so that we act as if it really doesn't hurt. But the Hebrew and biblical understanding of suffering is always corporate and accepted as redemptive. Paul described it as "completing" the redemptive activity of Christ.

I am sure that I do not understand all that suffering involves. How incredible that Paul would say that it is his "happiness" to "suffer." I cannot explain it, but I have seen it. My partner has demonstrated this quality throughout our shared life—and never more dramatically than she did at the time of my sickness and healing.

Discoveries on the Way

The greatest dramatization of the love that Christ has for the Church since Calvary is the love a man shows toward his wife. And the greatest dramatization of the appropriate response to that love by the Church is the respectful response that a wife returns to her husband. The husband-wife relationship, then, provides a potent evangelistic tool.

I really do want my children to be aware of and respond to the love that Christ has for His Church. I will gladly demonstrate that love by being kind to their mother.

Chapter 13
" 'Tis So Sweet To Trust In Jesus"

Sing thankfully in your hearts to God, with psalms and hymns and spiritual songs. Whatever you are doing, whether you speak or act, do everything in the name of the Lord Jesus, giving thanks to God the Father through him.

Colossians 3:16-17 (NEB)

I do not claim to comprehend the anatomy of a miracle. My intention in writing my story is not to impress people with what I know but to share what I have experienced. I will recount, as best I can, the events of the next few hours and describe the moments that preceded a totally unanticipated turn of events. I hope this story will strengthen faith in the goodness of God as a provider of miracles.

It really is "sweet to trust in Jesus" and to "take Him at His word."

Up to this point in my story, everything was rather bleak. The only hope the physicians offered for survival was a liver transplant, and by the most generous prediction, it had to be available in the next four days (I learned later that the average waiting time for a liver in the United States is 156 days). And even if a liver were available, my blood count would have had to improve dramatically if I were to survive surgery.

The Saturday following my flight back to Nashville was a very black day. Not even a fragment of memory of Saturday stays in my mind. But my family was very heavyhearted. I had survived the flight, but a whole new team of doctors was making new assessments of me. Family members were quizzed over and over again with questions that were, by that time, very familiar to them. "Yes, he has been healthy. No, he does not drink. No, he has not been in a foreign country in the last three months."

And the familiar questions evoked the same familiar conclusions from the doctors: "It is hepatitis A. It has gone fulminant. Enzyme counts are over 9,000. He must have a transplant soon. We have put him at the top of our transplant list." The doctors in Charleston had indicated my "window" for surgery was between six and eleven days. This was the seventh day. It was a bad day.

Fatigue was taking its toll on my family. These had been high-stress days. On the other hand, it was wonderful to have extended family members and friends to help. Barbara greeted our friends in the waiting room. She was better acquainted with the broader circle of members and friends than the children were. The children were allowed to be with me in intensive care more than they had been in Charleston, so they set up "shift duty." Martha's daughter, Lorri, who is a nurse by profession, had been keeping in touch with the Trevecca University nursing staff, and she and the school nurses tried to evaluate my condition. Together, they had grown very anxious. Time was passing. They tended to agree with the time estimates of the doctors in South Carolina. The seventh day was nearly over. They knew that a liver must be available very soon if I were to have any hope of survival.

Lorri took her "rotation" at my side. She described her time on Saturday with this sweet comment: "What I remember vividly is that even when you were 'not with us' you were calling out to God, 'Oh, Jesus, please help me. I am so sick.' You would ask me to pray for you, and you would tenderly reach out to hold my hand or touch my cheek. I remember that when the outcome looked very bleak there was still a peace and a joy surrounding the family—a quiet, Christlike calm which enabled us all to laugh and cry and know that God was sovereign." In her note she added, "I love you and I'm glad you are still here."

Early on Sunday. . .

I like stories that begin with the phrase "Early on Sunday." The greatest story ever told begins with these meaningful words, "Early on Sunday." For all my pastoral years, I had made it a point to be at the church by about six o'clock on Sunday mornings. There was something so very precious about being alone with the Lord and with my notes, which contained, I earnestly felt, His word for His people. I would routinely bring those people before the Lord in the light of the word He had called me to preach and ask Him to apply the word of comfort, instruction, conviction, rebuke, or healing to their hearts through my words. I know I was often praying for them as they still rested in their beds.

This Sunday morning was different. On this Sunday I was "resting." More accurately, I was unconscious on a hospital bed, and my people were praying for me. The mailings have convinced me that thousands of them were praying for me early on the first Sunday of March. On this Sunday they prayed for a word from the Lord for me. Many prayed that His word might be a word of intervention so that a liver might become available. A few have told me that they prayed for a word of healing: "Please, Lord, a word of healing for our brother!"

Here is my son Paul's account of what happened Sunday morning:

"On Sunday morning, March 3, Lisa and I arrived at the hospital for our 'shift.' We children decided that we needed to break the visiting time down into shifts because only two people were allowed to visit Dad in the intensive care unit. At this stage of his illness, he could not identify his children nor was he cognizant of his surroundings. Unknown to us, Dad had been very agitated throughout Saturday night—even pulling I-Vs out of his arm. When we saw him that morning, he was in restraints, both arms firmly tied to the bed because of the long night's struggle. He didn't recognize me or my wife of twelve years. Since my father had enjoyed excellent health throughout his life, seeing him in this helpless state was very hard for me to deal with emotionally.

"That morning Lisa thought it would be a good idea to bring a tape of favorite hymns set to classical music. She thought the music might be soothing as well as familiar. Upon our arrival, Dad seemed to be awake and talked with us about the terrible night that he had had, but he spoke to us as if we were strangers. He looked through me with no recognition.

"When the music began, I didn't think he heard it initially. It was only when the old song "Tis So Sweet to Trust in Jesus,' mixed with the beautiful 'Claire de Lune' by Debussy, began that he started to sing the familiar hymn: 'Jesus, Jesus, how I trust Him! How I've proved Him o'er and o'er! Jesus, Jesus, precious Jesus! Oh, for grace to trust Him more!'

"He then looked at the two of us and asked, 'Did I do okay?' Lisa and I began to cry and said, 'Yes, you did fine, Dad.' At that moment, the cardiologist came into the room. He saw Lisa and me crying and asked if everything was all right. I knew then that everything really was going to be all right. The three of us prayed, and after the prayer, Dad called us by name. That was the first time he had recognized either of us since his arrival at Vanderbilt. Lisa called my brothers and sister to tell them of Dad's positive report. I stayed in his room and thanked God for His wonderful grace and mercy."

I just love this story. I so wish I could remember its happening. I have tried to convince Paul that he heard me sing the second verse: "Oh, how sweet to trust in Jesus, Just to trust His cleansing blood; Just in simple faith to plunge me 'Neath the HEALING, cleansing flood!"

He says, in full honesty, that he cannot remember. He only knows that I seemed to be singing my confession of faith.

Throughout that Lord's Day morning, precious friends in congregations across the nations were holding me up to the Lord in prayer. In my home congregation, a statement prepared by my family the evening before was read by Pastor Henecke:

> The Reed Family would like to sincerely thank all the people for their constant thoughts and prayers. Dad has acute hepatitis A, and the doctors and the family are hoping that his liver will fight off the infection and that his body will heal itself, but this is a waiting game.
>
> The doctors tell us that we must get a positive sign in the next few days. Will you continue to pray for our father's health and for the family? We will update the information lines at First Church and Trevecca as additional information is made known to us. As you can understand, only family members are permitted into an ICU room to visit Dad.
>
> The Scripture promises, and Dad has said to us so many times, that God will not forsake us. He is always faithful.
>
> In lieu of flowers and plants, Dad has requested dona-tions be made to the President's Scholarship Fund at Trevecca Nazarene University. The last line sounds like Dad, doesn't it?

Then Pastor Henecke prayed:

> I come to you today, my God, as a spokesman in the house of the Lord, and I come to you as the shepherd of the flock. You can hear all our souls; you know our spirits; you know collectively what is going on in this room.
>
> But our prayer focuses on what is happening on the seventh floor of Vanderbilt University Hospital. We pray for a specific room there, Lord, in the ICU ward, and we pray today not for **Dr.** Millard Reed or for **Pastor** or **President** Reed. We are praying for your servant and our brother,

Millard Reed. And we are praying, "Heal in the name of Jesus."

We lift to you your daughter Barbara and all the family. I name to you today, Lord, Steve, Deborah, Paul, John, and the grandkids. And we pray, God, keep the family united and continue the healing process that is going on in our brother.

Lord, you know all about Trevecca, and you know all its needs. So we pray for every administrator, and we pray for all the faculty. Hold them steady, Lord.

And I thank you today for the gospel.

And I thank you, God, for Millard Reed. Continue, we pray, to war against disease in that body. In Jesus' name, Amen.

The family did not tell the people of my early Sunday morning songfest.

On Sunday afternoon I returned to genuine consciousness as I describe in the first chapter of this book. From that point on, I had full continuity of thought. My temperature had begun to move back toward normal, and the enzyme count was falling. Late that night I sang again and I remember doing so. I sang intentionally, "I sing praises to your name, Oh Lord." I was sensing my return.

On Tuesday I was placed in a private room. I told Barbara that moving me was a mistake. The room was arranged in such a way that I could see myself in a mirror from my bed. What a frightening figure: yellow, gaunt, frail. "I look like death warmed over," I said. "I accept the 'warmed over' part. I am just glad you are here," she responded.

On Wednesday I was up and walking, though hesitantly at first. On Thursday I went home. Dr. Burk said he wanted to see me on the following Monday. In the next chapter I will share what he had to say in that meeting.

As I rested at home on Thursday, some of my forgotten memories began to return to me. I especially began to recall my preaching from Colossians to the folks there at St. Andrews in Charleston. When Paul told me about my Sunday morning "song service" in intensive care, I thought of the apostle's admonition to his spiritual grandchildren in Colossae: "Sing thankfully in your hearts to God, with psalms and hymns and spiritual songs" (Col. 3:16).

As I have gathered and reflected upon the various details of my healing, I have come to the persuasion that the time of "thankful singing" "early on Sunday morning" was the turning point in my recovery. It seemed to be the time that God identified as the moment of return. It really is "sweet to trust in Jesus" and to "take Him at His word."

<hr />

Discoveries on the Way

All healing comes from God. Sometimes scientists can explain a healing as "natural" because the improvement is predictable.

From time to time, the healing is beyond the explanation of the scientists. This type of healing we are inclined to call "miraculous." It is perceived by us to be more dramatic than other types, but all healing is from God.

The ultimate healing will be in our glorification at the article of our death. Any healing before that is temporary and partial.

But when I stand before the King, my body will be without a blemish, a reflection of His own glorified body. Hallelujah!

Chapter 14
"Our Dear Friend, The Doctor"

Greetings to you from our dear friend Luke, the doctor.
Colossians 4:14 (NEB)

Dr. Burk's voice had summoned me back from dark oblivion on Sunday afternoon. He is the one whom I asked to repeat all of those questions about where I was, what I did, and who I was, and to provide the correct answers. And when his answers brought me back to reality, I embraced them as a drowning man might cling to a piece of driftwood.

> *"I have made a presentation of your case to a medical conference here at Vanderbilt, and I entitled it 'A Remarkable Recovery.'"*

When he walked in very early on Monday morning, I recognized him and said with as much gusto as I could muster in that weak condition, "You are Dr. Burk!" He seemed amused with my obvious sense of accomplishment and sat at my bedside to talk awhile.

My mind was not yet fully clear, and I struggled to catch what he was telling me. "You have been very sick," he told me, "very, very sick. But you are now better, considerably better. We are glad for that," he said. "But you might relapse and be very sick again," he went on. "But I don't want you to worry about that."

Even with my limited keenness of mind, I thought, "This man is talking in circles. If he doesn't want me to worry about a relapse, why is he even telling me about the possibility?"

When I visited his office for the first time on the following Monday, he asked me a lot of questions about my health, about my work, and about my faith. Barbara and Melvin had accompanied me so that they could hear his instructions about my activities during convalescence.

After the lengthy conversation, in which I was able to share in spite of a voice that was still very weak, he said, "I need to tell you that your liver died and that your body is regenerating a new liver spontaneously. More specifically, three pounds of tissue has died within you, and you are in the process of regenerating three pounds of new tissue. We can expect the regeneration to take six to eight weeks."

My first response was, "That's about as close to having a baby as a man can come." He smiled. "But what is happening to that dead tissue?" I asked.

"There are scavenger cells in your body which clean up that dead tissue and reprocess the protein. Normally, the body cannot process that much tissue. The fact that your body has successfully done so is one of the amazing things about your story."

"Isn't all of this pretty rare?" I asked.

"Yes, but it is not totally unheard of."

"What was your assessment of me when I arrived here at Vanderbilt?"

"I would have given you no better than a 50-50 chance for survival WITH a transplant. Far, far less without a transplant." He added, "Far, far less."

"What medicines did you give me to aid in my recovery?"

"We have no medicine to heal hepatitis when it has gone fulminant. We were giving you vitamin K in an all-out effort to prepare your blood for surgery in the event that a liver became available."

We sat quietly for a moment or two. Then I broke the silence: "My people think it is a miracle!"

Dr. Burk had been very kind to me. His manner was gentle. His voice had called me back from the "darkness." His voice was still soft, nearly subdued. "Well, we doctors use that word a little differently. We see things every day that some would call a miracle. I will tell you this: I have made a presentation of your case to a medical conference here at Vanderbilt, and I entitled it 'A Remarkable Recovery.'"

Our Monday conversation helped me understand better his earlier tentative warning of relapse. The readings that he had been taking from me were almost too good to be true. He wanted to be fair with me and not build up a false optimism.

As I write this material, more than a year has passed. There has been no hint of any relapse. My recovery has been swift and uninterrupted, and I have returned to full health and energy. In fact, during my few office visits, I have commented to the doctor that possibly my new liver might be even better than my old one was. My old one had inclined me toward an elevated triglyceride count, a problem for which I had taken medication for two years. He suggested that such an improvement would be a bit much to expect. Six months later I received my first full blood count since my illness. The triglyceride count was down by over two hundred points. The doctor will not concede the point, but I think my new liver is better than my old one. That is what I think. I KNOW that God does all things well.

I am deeply grateful to the extended team of physicians who cared for me during my illness. The only ones I really remember are Drs. Hazell and Rashford in Charleston and Dr. Burk in Nashville. But I am obliged to all of them—even the lady doctor with the South American accent who so troubled Barbara. I have worked with physicians throughout my pastoral years. Their role is impossibly difficult, and often, as was true in my case, there is very little that they can do but attend to the patient and try to keep him or her comfortable. From time to time, they see miracles and are as awed as we are. Maybe more so.

As I was recuperating at home and reflecting on their care, Colossians 4:14 came to my mind: "Greetings to you from our dear friend Luke, the doctor." The doctors were able to do very little in my case, but they are my friends, and I am indebted to all of them for their kind care.

———— • ᛝ ᛡ ᛝ • ————

Discoveries on the Way

Every mortal being, every animal, every insect, and microbe is a testimony of the creative work of God. We are created by Him whether we are aware of His creative act or not.

Some persons, gifted with mental skills to explore the details of this grand creation, also get the opportunity to do so. These persons gain insights into the creation that assist in its continuation and so propagate life.

I am deeply respectful of those who have such gifts and opportunity and take advantage of them for the betterment of mankind.

The deeper awe is reserved for "THE ONE" who is the power of creation with its continuing vitality.

Chapter 15
Flowers From God

He was supreme in the beginning and—leading the resurrection parade—he is supreme in the end. From beginning to end he's there, towering far above everything, everyone. So spacious is he, so roomy, that everything of God finds its proper place in him without crowding. Not only that, but all the broken and dislocated pieces of the universe—people and things, animals and atoms—get properly fixed and fit together in vibrant harmonies, all because of his death, his blood that poured down from the Cross.
Colossians 1:18-20 (*The Message*)

Dr. Burk had indicated that the creation of new tissue in my body would take all my energy, leaving me with very little for daily routine. I found that his prediction was correct. For the first three or four weeks I gave a major portion of my day to bed rest.

Such welcomed quiet time gave me pleasant opportunity for reflection. I drank it in, enjoying every aspect of it. At least that was true for the first couple of weeks. During that time, I began to learn how truly ill I had been as the family shared stories of which I had no memory. It began to dawn on me that I had not only been ill but that I had been ill unto death. Slowly, I began to learn of the doctor's prognosis that left virtually no room for a medical cure. Gradually, I began to realize that what had transpired in my body was a "miracle." Healing, I began to see, was not only a "promise from God" and an article of my faith, it was a very specific reality in my very own body.

God wants us to know of His benevolence. He is our Father who finds delight in doing good things for us, His children.

My first mood was one of celebration. I rejoiced in everything. A late spring snowfall decorated the trees just outside my bedroom window. How beautiful it was. Crocuses were already dotting the lawn, and soon redbud was in bloom. Nature seemed to be celebrating new life with me.

How beautiful each member of my family appeared, especially my granddaughters. When Stephen and Diane brought Elizabeth and Ashley to see me, I hugged them tightly and listened to the melody of their childish voices. When Deborah and her Stephen brought Sarah and Rebecca, the girls stood back from me for a moment, trying to take me in. Sarah said, "Where's my grandpa?" She was kidding, of course. Her joke was her way of commenting on how frail I looked. Rebecca, a high school junior, cried as we talked about how good God had been in sparing my life. Soon they were both at my side and in my arms, and we hugged with all our energy. How sweet it was to feel their embrace one more time. Life was good.

I seemed to have a new awareness that everything is a blessing to be celebrated. The family. The house. The food brought in by neighbors. A brief walk in the yard. God had healed me. All these blessings I had very nearly lost. But the Heavenly Father had restored them, and I was happy in my heart. After my pattern, I would break out in song upon my bed. Sometimes, during the day. Sometimes, in the night. Barbara didn't mind. She celebrated with me.

I should have known that the mood might change. I had been a pastor long enough and walked alongside enough ill persons that I should have been prepared for what would follow. I was not. Once again I learned that it is one thing to be alongside a bed and quite another to be in the bed.

My sense of oppression may have begun about the third week. (A doctor might call it depression, but I am being kind to myself.) As it became clearer to me that I had missed death by the narrowest of margins, and that only by the healing providence of God, I began to ask, "Why me? Why should God have spared me? Why me and not Julie? Why me and not Amy? Does God play favorites? Do I like a God who plays favorites even if I am the one favored?"

Maybe such questioning was the result of too much time for reflection. Maybe my weakness made me a prime target for Satan. Maybe those are legitimate questions that need to be answered.

I tried to create adequate answers, but I could not. "Maybe God has something special for me to do!" was my first thought. But then I immediately reasoned, "Well, that may or may not be true, but didn't God have something for Julie to do also?" Julie had been a part of my church during her college years and even then was a "saint" in my opinion. As a college student, she had organized "King's Kids" in the nearby housing projects and loved and cared for the children of poverty. And when she and Greg married, they ministered side by side. When their girls were born, the ministry team just got bigger. Then one day while playing in the snow with her girls, she felt a pain that sent her to the doctor. In spite of volumes of prayer and her sweet, saintly testimony indicating her faith in God, she died ten months later leaving Greg, now a professor on my faculty, to care for those darling little girls—without her help. DIDN'T GOD HAVE SOMETHING FOR JULIE TO DO? It seemed obvious to me that He did. My oppression was not lighter. It was heavier.

"But what about the great volume of prayer on my behalf? Maybe that is why God healed me," I thought. How could I be anything but grateful for prayer? I couldn't even pray for myself, at least not consciously. I was totally dependent upon the prayers of others. But does God have a scale by which He measures the total "weight" of prayers sent up for each one so that when the scale "tips" in the right direction a bell sounds and that prayer is answered? I couldn't accept that reasoning. That description doesn't sound like the God I know. Even if such a scheme were true, and I can't believe that it is, both Julie and Amy would have tipped the scales long before I did. That theory doesn't make sense.

Precious Amy was the beloved teenage daughter of missionaries Jerry and Tony Porter. She was prayed for by the world from the time her cancer was discovered. Christians prayed faithfully for Amy through a whole series of awful examinations and surgeries over several years. Yet, she died within weeks of her prayed-for and longed-for wedding. Is God a sadist? Does He taunt us? Why would Julie be taken with a whole life of service before her? Why Amy, younger yet and the object of worldwide prayer? Why should I be healed? Most of my ministry had already been done. I lay in my bed thinking that God had not done well in His choice for healing. Better to heal either one of these young ladies than me.

Two weeks or so of these ponderings were giving me a heavy, heavy heart. God had been very good to me. I was deeply grateful. But I found myself questioning His character. He obviously is able to heal. It is just as obvious that He does not always do so. "So who's to blame?" I thought. "Is God to blame?" I can't believe that. "Are the saints to blame? Is the fault a lack of prayer? Or a lack of faith?" No,

I had rejected that theory years ago when Kenny Taylor had died. "Is it the fault of the ill person?" I had people suggest that I was healed because of all the good work I had done over the years. I knew better than that. God does not work that way. He does not fault us for failing to make it across some invisible goal line of good works. I just didn't understand. And my spirit, which should have been jubilant, was laden with oppression.

As the April weather grew pleasant, I began to go for walks in our community—down our long driveway some one hundred yards, then left past Byron and Jennie's house, up past Rosebank School, and back again. A walk along this route would take me twenty minutes or so. I was refreshed and invigorated as I sensed some strength returning.

As I walked I took my questions along with me. They were especially heavy on my mind the third Sunday of April. It was almost six o'clock in the evening, a familiar time throughout my life. For thirty-five years, that was the time that I was all geared up to deliver my evening message and, by the grace of God, meet seekers at the altar and lead them to Jesus. I had always relished that high-energy time.

Now, here I was trudging along in a weak body, trying to grow a new liver and regain enough strength to function again. Furthermore, I was agonizing over what I felt I had discovered as a "character flaw" in the nature of God.

As I returned to my drive, I chose to go up the drive around my neighbor Bob's house rather than by way of my own driveway. His drive went among the big elms and oaks that had just formed their delicate, pale green leaves of spring. As I walked I recalled what Jesus had said about considering the lilies of the field and the sparrows of the air.

About two-thirds of the way up Bob's drive, where it bends to the left and is shadowed by the big trees, I came upon an extraordinarily lovely patch of wild flowers about the size of a bathtub. They were exquisitely and delicately beautiful in shades of lavender and white. I remember them from my childhood; back then the old ladies called them "lily-belles." They are "columbine." I could not help stopping for a while to drink in the beauty. The long rays of the setting sun penetrated the woods and caressed my pastoral scene with just enough light to make it perfect. I stood transfixed for a minute or two, maybe three.

Then, from the upper right-hand corner of my idyllic picture, a bumblebee with amazing speed did an exaggerated three-hundred-

and-sixty degree circle dead center in my view and went buzzing off to the left and was gone. It startled me, but I instantly accepted that bee as the signature of God. We all know that it is aeronautically impossible for a bumblebee to fly. Its body is too heavy and its wings are too short for flight. Its doing the impossible before my very eyes prepared me to hear the voice of God.

"That bumblebee flies because I tell it to," I heard God say. "I sent it to catch your attention. And I have regenerated this flowerbed as I do each spring. I did it without your help or the help of any other mortal. Regeneration is what I do, and regenerating a new liver for you is no big deal." I began to weep, but God was not finished. "You are inclined to make idols, and you have made an idol of the rational mind. Now, bring that idol, as you must bring all your idols, and lay it at the foot of my throne. I alone am sovereign." My weeping became sobs of submission.

How pleasant His voice was as He said, "I am also benevolent. I chide you as I did Job and ask, 'Where were you when I built the universe and formed the land and seas?'" My sobs were subsiding, and I began to drift toward laughter. And once He got me in a playful mood, He said (I received this message as a word of the Lord as clear as any I have ever received), "I saw you in your misery and nudged one of the heavenly host and said to him, 'Well, there is Millard. What shall we do? Tell you what, let's just heal him. It will be fun to watch him as he tries to figure it all out.'"

I laughed out loud. Throughout my ministry, I had emphasized the sovereignty of God, and He had just reemphasized it to me. But He also wants us to know of His benevolence. He is our Father who finds delight in doing good things for us, His children.

As I walked the remaining hundred or so yards back to our house, my heart was light again. God had summoned me to lay down my idol and then, as my sovereign, was pleased to kid me about my recovery. He is my friend.

As I greeted Barbara in our family room, I began to weep again. "What's wrong, Honey?" she asked. "Are you feeling bad?"

"No, I feel wonderful! The Father has made himself known to me, and my heart is light."

I soon found my way back to Colossians and read Paul's words: "Through him God chose to reconcile the whole universe to himself, making peace through the shedding of His blood upon the cross—to reconcile all things, WHETHER ON EARTH OR IN HEAVEN, THROUGH HIM ALONE" (Col.1:20).

The "whole universe" includes a patch of "lily-belles," a bumble-bee, and my heavy heart. My heart needed peace. A bumblebee delivered "flowers from God" with a good-natured note that said "Peace." He hinted later that my one appropriate response is "Thank you!" I have been saying it often. I say it again now. "Thank you, Heavenly Father! It is a joy to be your child."

Discoveries on the Way

Depression is not necessarily an indication of spiritual sickness. Often the most spiritually mature find themselves with a heavy heart as they struggle to understand the work and character of God.

The "struggle to understand" is a noble effort often blessed by profound new insight. But from time to time it exhausts itself in futile insistence that the rational mind be pacified. Such an insistence makes an idol of the mind. Like all idolatry, it must be shattered so that the one and only sovereign may be acknowledged.

I resign all my idols to my God.

Chapter 16
Heaven Is Real

When Christ, who is our life, is manifested, then you too will be manifested with him in glory.

Colossians 3:4 (NEB)

The "fresh aroma" that wafted over my spirit from the "flowers from God" had the fragrance of heaven within it. Let me explain.

At issue in all my mental anguish was the character of God. More especially crucial was the question of His goodness. I was confident of His sovereignty, but His goodness seemed to be in question. He had been good to me. But what of others?

> *Heaven is the land of God's goodness beyond this life.*

I somehow knew that His goodness could not hinge on His healing of my body. It cannot hinge on the healing of those prayed for, because He doesn't heal all who are prayed for. He didn't heal Kenny. He didn't heal Julie or Amy. And one day, He may not heal me. I was healed. I was not resurrected.

As I had walked up Bob's driveway, before my rendezvous with the bumblebee, I had been wondering, "Would God have been good to Barbara even if I had died?" I thought of my dear, lifetime friend, Dwight Millikan, who died suddenly at the age of fifty-four. Was God good to his wife, Marilyn? Well, yes, although her sorrow was painful, God was good to her and their children. I believe that God would also have been good to Barbara had I died. She has great strength and determination. Her spiritual depth would have provided resources adequate for her day. And the children would have been good to her.

And He would have been good to our children. They are adults now and capable people who are well along in their professions. God would have been good to them in my absence.

He would have been good to the University also. I had enjoyed five years as its president, and the school had experienced good progress with many plans for the future in place. Dean Pusey told me that one of the things I said to him when he came to see me was, "Well, this was not a part of our strategic plan was it?" It would have taken a few months (maybe weeks) to find a new president, but God would have been good to the University if I had died. He always has been. I had no doubt about His faithful goodness to the school.

The key question that was working my mind was "Would God have been good to ME had I died?" The heart of the matter is my answer to these questions: Do I believe in heaven? Do I really believe that, had I drifted out of unconsciousness in the other direction rather than back in this direction, I would have been in the presence of the King? Would I have been greeted by my dear mother and father? Would they have introduced me to my sister, Elnora, who had died as an infant before I was born? Would Robert and Charles Phillip, my older brothers, have been there?" Other names and faces passed through my mind. I thought of dear ones who had borne the burden of kingdom work alongside me through the years, people who had loved me with unmixed affection and whose deaths I had grieved as deeply as I would have the death of a family member. Would we have joined in sweet fellowship there? Do I believe that? Can I, a twentieth-century man, accept a first-century cosmology?

Can Paul possibly be right when he tells the Colossians (2:15), "And he exists before everything, and **all things** are held together in him"? And "Every power and authority in the universe is subject to him as Head" (2:1). And again, "When Christ, who is our life, is manifested, **then you too will be manifested with him in glory**" (3:4).

My rational mind was asking, "Can I believe that? Really? Not just as a familiar song to sing or a pleasant comfort to pass along to the bereaved? Had I made 'the journey,' do I believe that heaven would have awaited me there?" These were my thoughts as I started up Bob's driveway.

And then I encountered God in an emotional, less-than-rational way, and I heard Him say, "You have made an idol of the rational mind. Bring it and place it at the foot of my throne. Believe that I am sovereign and that I am good. I would have been good to you had you died, and I am good to you as you remain in this life for a while. I intend you to enjoy my blessings in this life and in the life to come."

Now here I am, a man who has spent his life in the pursuit of the cultivation of the rational mind, trying to explain (in some way that may make sense to other rational beings) that a patch of flowers and a bumblebee enabled me to hear the kindly voice of my Heavenly Father assuring me of His loving care. How ridiculous! How **wonderfully** ridiculous—like Abram's hearing a voice calling him to leave his country, or Moses' seeing a bush that burned but was not consumed, or Isaiah's seeing the Lord as His train filled the temple.

Heaven is real! I know there is the Hubble space telescope which now provides sights into deep space and black holes and stellar blowouts. But then again, there are bumblebees and "lily-belles" along Bob's driveway, and Sunday evening sunlight in spring, and fresh, pale green leaves, and a weary preacher with a new liver in his body, hearing God offer fellowship much as He had to Adam in the cool of the evening.

We mortals have difficulty accepting the heavenly. We want to understand it. He asks us to receive it. And when we do receive it, we are slow to apply it to our lives. We want to go to heaven but not on this afternoon's bus.

It is my duty to represent the University at twelve different district assemblies of the Church of the Nazarene. I was sufficiently strong enough to attend that series including the assembly in Orlando, Florida, in May following my illness. Superintendent and Mrs. Gene Fuller are my long-time friends from college days, so I especially looked forward to being with them. I always look forward to Central Florida because "they really do things up big." Maybe a bit of Disney World rubs off.

At this evening session the huge auditorium was packed to the back wall. The faithful were there to be blessed. The theme was heaven, and a large choir accompanied by an orchestra sang many of our favorite songs about heaven. Along the way, the congregation joined in singing "How Beautiful Heaven Must Be!" Some of the saints revived a practice of an earlier year and walked the aisles in holy joy. It was a gracious, Christ-anointed service and especially meaningful to me.

But then, at the end of the service, the superintendent introduced me. As I stood to step forward, the place erupted in thunderous applause. Every church represented there that night had prayed for me. Many had designated someone to represent me and had anointed that person on my behalf. All had heard the bad, bad news of imminent death. Many of them knew me personally. Most of them were seeing me for the first time since my illness. They stood and clapped their hands and lifted praise to God. I was deeply, deeply moved.

After the service, Trevecca's director of alumni services, Dale Killingsworth, said with a sheepish smile on his face, "Did that service seem a little strange to you?" "Why would you ask?" I responded. "Well, we spent the first fifty minutes celebrating heaven and expressing our longing to go there, and then we spent the last ten minutes rejoicing because our dear friend **DID NOT GO**. We should have said, 'Sorry, better luck next time!' "

I did not have a "white-light," near-death experience that some have described. Often such persons indicate that they no longer have any fear of death. I cannot claim that. In fact, my enriched appreciation for life makes me all the more disinclined to want to leave. I love this life which, through Christ, is "abundant." I am not eager to depart. The time may come when I will long for my heavenly home. I know that my mother did in her late years. But for now, I really am happy here and view death not as a friend but as an enemy.

But since "the flight of the bumblebee," I am confident that God is sovereign AND that He is good. All who accept His sovereignty will also enjoy His goodness in this life and in the life to come.

Discoveries on the Way

God is good! He is good in all situations and to all people. He was good in providing healing to my body. BUT HIS GOODNESS DID NOT HINGE ON HIS HEALING OF MY BODY. Had I died, He still would have been good to my family, to my friends, and to me.

Heaven is the land of God's goodness beyond this life. Jesus promised it; I believe it. I will enjoy His blessings there someday.

Chapter 17
To See As God Sees

The Father. . . has made you fit to share the heritage of God's people in the realm of light.

Colossians 1:12 (NEB)

I must share one more fascinating experience before completing my story.

Earlier I described how Kathy Parker's face seemed to be the face of an angel when she visited me in South Carolina. More specifically, her face was not only beautiful, but it seemed to radiate as if illuminated with light from within. The whole of her countenance seemed awash with a glorious glow. I cannot know what the children of Israel saw when the face of Moses shone so brightly before them that they had to place a veil over it. But I think I viewed something of a similar Shekinah on that Monday when Kathy visited me as I was beginning to lose consciousness.

> *I continue to look at God's children with new eyes. This new way of seeing God's people is one of the benefits of my illness.*

A parallel thing happened as I began to return to awareness on the following Sunday. The first person that I happened to see was my daughter, Debbie, who was at my bedside. As her face came into my view, she said, "Hi, Daddy," and smiled. She was wondrously beautiful. I mean, make-you-cry beautiful. And her beauty was more than the earthly kind. As Kathy's face had glowed from an inner radiance, so now Debbie's face was awash with what appeared to be a heavenly light. As I turned to see Paul and Lisa, the same glory surrounded them. But that aura of glory around my loved ones seemed to diminish as I regained normal consciousness.

Were these visions simply the products of my joy in the rediscovery of my loving family and friend? Possibly they were the illusions of a fevered mind? I really don't know for sure. These visions give me reason to ponder.

In my teaching and preaching I have always emphasized the importance of having a vision of God. During the years that I have taught pastoral theology, I have routinely asked the students to go with me in our shared thoughts to Caesarea Philippi where Jesus asks His disciples who they claim Him to be. Peter responds, "You are the Christ, the Son of the living God." And immediately our Lord blesses him. His confession is sound. His doctrine is "orthodox."

But very soon, when Peter rebukes the Lord for speaking of suffering, Jesus calls him "Satan," a "devil," not because of a theological deviation but because his perspective is wrong. The *Williams New Testament* translates our Lord's words in Matthew 16:23: "FOR YOU LOOK AT THINGS NOT AS GOD DOES BUT AS MAN DOES." "Orthodoxy is not enough," I have said to prospective young pastors. "You must see things as God sees them. YOU MUST HAVE THE EYES OF GOD." The rest of our school year, indeed the rest of our lives, is spent in coming to grips with this audacious demand. But we never get around it; we must have the eyes of God if we are to minister in His name.

My reflection time, since my healing, has enabled me to see that the Bible is not primarily a book of theology. It is not primarily a book filled with ideas ABOUT God. It includes some ideas about God, but they are not its most obvious message.

The Bible is a book of theophony. It contains the vision of God. It is filled with accounts of those who SAW THE LORD and found their sight transformed by that epiphany. The heart of the Scriptures is not theology but theophony.

Before sin entered the world, Adam and Eve had fellowship with God on a daily basis. Enoch walked with God, and God took him. Abram heard the voice and obeyed. Jacob wrestled with the Lord in the night and was transformed. Moses heard the voice from the burning bush. Isaiah saw the Lord high and lifted up and was commissioned. All of these men caught a vision of God.

The New Testament story is very similar. At the coming of Jesus, the shepherds saw the angels, and the wise men saw the star.

Jesus' public ministry began with Philip's saying to Nathanael, "Come and see" (John 1:46)—and ended with the disciples' declaring, "We have seen the Lord!" (John 20:25). And when the resurrected Jesus ascended, the two men in white apparel said to those gazing up into heaven, "This same Jesus...will come back in the same way you have seen him go into heaven (Acts 1:11). Early in John's writings he testifies, "We have seen his glory" (John 1:14).

And late in his ministry he would write, "...we have seen with our eyes, which we have looked at" (I John 1:1). When he, by the inspiration of the Spirit, predicts the last day he says, "...every eye will see him" (Rev. 1:7).

Paul's vision near Damascus (Acts 9:4), the call from Macedonia (Acts 16:9), and the angel that appeared in the night aboard ship (Acts 27:23) further make the point that the Scripture is filled with the accounts of those who experienced a vision of God. It is the vision that transforms their sight and inspires them to serve.

To each of these and many others God made himself known, and those who saw Him were never the same. Their whole way of looking at things changed. They began to assume the eyes of God, to see things as He sees them.

I am not dogmatic about my visions of Kathy, Debbie, Paul, and Lisa. I just know that they were radiantly beautiful in my eyes. And I am inclined to think that I saw them, in some measure, as God sees them. When I expressed my opinion to Kathy, she began to cry. "Do you mean that you think God sees me as beautiful?" she asked.

I told her, "If my poor, limited brain could see that wondrous beauty for just a few seconds, I am confident that the Lord of the universe sees with unblinking eyes and beholds the glory of His own image within you." My response was an expression of my deepest-held conviction that His goodness bathes us in His own beauty, and we are glorious in His sight. I fear that we, who have tended to emphasize His condemnation of us, have difficulty in accepting His benevolence. Clearly, the Father finds great joy in His children. We are His children and He sees us as beautiful.

The apostle comments in Colossians, "The Father has made you fit to share...the heritage of God's people in the realm of light." I have prayed that something of His perspective might remain with me as I look upon His children. To some considerable degree, I think I continue to look at His children with new eyes. This new way of seeing God's people is one of the benefits of my illness.

• ╫═◄●❁●►═╫ •

Discoveries on the Way

When the writer of the ancient story provides the words of creation for us, they are "LET THERE BE LIGHT!" Contemporary scientists tell us that they have no more precise description of creation than that one. Light is the basic energy of the universe.

The Scripture is laced with various illuminations of light as expressions of the presence of God. The burning bush, the shining face, the glory surrounding the angels—each is seen by mortals as the vision of God.

I will ask God for eyes to see Him in His glory. I will also ask to see as He sees. He gives us a new way of seeing things, the true paradigm shift.

Chapter 18
If Your Door Has Not Yet Opened

You are not to be disqualified by the decision of people who go in for self-mortification and angel-worship, and try to enter into some vision of their own. Such people, bursting with the futile conceit of worldly minds, lose hold upon the Head; yet it is from the Head that the whole body, with all its joints and ligaments, receives its supplies, and thus knit together grows according to God's design.

Colossians 2:18-19 (NEB)

Don't tolerate people who try to run your life, ordering you to bow and scrape, insisting that you join their obsession with angels and that you seek out visions. They're a lot of hot air, that's all they are. They're completely out of touch with the source of life, Christ, who puts us together in one piece, whose very breath and blood flow through us. He is the Head and we are the body. We can grow up healthy in God only as he nourishes us.

Colossians 2:18-19 (*The Message*)

I received my "flowers from God" on the third Sunday of April alongside my neighbor's driveway. I remember how oppressed I had been before they came to my attention and how relieved I felt afterward. They changed my life.

As I have worked through this story, I have been very aware, all along, that some of you who read it may not have yet received your flowers from God. Your feelings are much more like my "pre-bumblebee" feelings rather than like my later feelings, after I received my flowers from God. Your interest in this book may be sparked by a desperate hope that somewhere within its pages you might find your "bouquet." Some of you have suffered a long time and find a certain lack of fairness in the

> *You must remember that your present painful circumstances are not indicative of some flaw in your relationship with your Heavenly Father. He still loves you.*

fact that my story reports a relatively brief period of suffering.

I have been very aware of the disparity between my situation and that of others—even Barbara, my wife, as I have written. You may have noticed in my story that Barbara has been suffering long-term pain in her back. Four vertebrae low in her spine have assumed an awkward random position. "It is a congenital arthritic back," the doctors say, "and surgery will not be of help. Epidural shots may provide some relief, or you may have to learn how to deal with pain more effectively."

Barbara and I have discussed this disparity as we have thought about you. Many of you are our personal friends, and many others are now acquainted with us by way of our shared story. And we know that some of you are continuing to suffer pain. "Many of our friends are much worse off than I am," Barbara has said to me. "Many have suffered much longer."

To those of you "who have not yet received your flowers from God," I want you to know of my sympathy and Barbara's understanding. You want to rejoice with me in my healing but wonder sometimes why the Heavenly Father, who you agree is kind, has not yet expressed that special kindness to you. You continue in your pain. And Satan, or some who unwittingly assist him, causes you to think that God has forgotten you or that you are no longer His "beautiful child."

You must remember that your present painful circumstances are not indicative of some flaw in your relationship with your Heavenly Father. He still loves you. An experience which I had during my second autumn at Trevecca illustrates my point.

I had not been president very long, and I think I was still acting very much like a pastor in that I scheduled things too tightly. I had agreed to welcome a visiting conference at a dinner meeting at 5:45 p.m., provide a brief orientation for a new class of adult learners at 6:00 p.m., and preach for the nearby Hermitage congregation at 7:00 p.m. Doable, but tight.

I greeted the dinner meeting, snatched a few bites of food, and was moving through the Jernigan Student Center toward the adult learners at exactly 6:00 p.m. As I breezed past the elevator door, it opened of its own accord, and I stepped in, thinking I could save ten seconds, maybe, toward the third floor.

The door closed, and I pushed the button marked "3." Nothing happened. I pushed again. Nothing! So I pushed the "Open Door" button. Nothing! I frantically pushed random buttons—anything that would free me from this "box." Nothing worked. No movement.

Rational man that I am, I reasoned that the elevator might work on gears that might be "dead center." "If I just jump up and down," I thought, "maybe I can jar it into action." I jumped up and down. The elevator shook but did not move to release me. I stopped, fearing that the whole box would jar loose and go crashing to the bottom.

I had not wanted to call for help. Calling would have been so "undignified" for a college president. But my watch read 6:03 p.m., and I was getting desperate. I reached for the little door that said "phone," but there was no phone in the compartment. There was an empty Luden's cough drop box. I visualized some unfortunate predecessor who may have lost his or her voice calling for help.

I turned quickly to the red "emergency" button with some fear that it might not work either. But it worked. It rang—and rang and rang. And no one took time to pay any attention to a wayward bell ringing on and on at 6:10 p.m. in the dining hall.

I wondered if I could turn it off as well as on and found I could. I tried to think of my Boy Scout days when I learned a bit of Morse code, but all I could remember was the signal for victory: dot, dot, dot, dash. It had been a long time since World War II. I cast that message aside in favor of the tempo of some familiar church song. Soon I was playing the tempo of "Victory in Jesus" on the emergency alarm.

As I was about halfway through the second verse of "Victory in Jesus," I heard the voice of one of our female students say, "Are you in there?"

"Well, I haven't gone anyplace!" I responded. The first phase of claustrophobia had begun to sweep over me.

"Who are you?" she asked.

I am very hesitant to use my title on campus. It sounds so officious to me. But at that moment of desperation, I was willing to use all the authority I could muster. "I am President Reed!" I said as "officially" as I could.

"OH, YOU ARE NOT!" she said in a scoffing tone. "WHO ARE YOU REALLY?"

"WELL, WHOEVER I AM" (I was near second-phase claustrophobia) "I WANT OUT OF HERE!" She disappeared. It was after 6:10 p.m., and I thought, "It looks as if I will spend the night in this 'box.'"

But pretty soon, she was back. "I forgot to tell you that I went for help," she said. By 6:15 p.m. the maintenance crew had discovered that the trouble was a circuit breaker. The door opened automatically, and as I walked out, my teenage rescuer said in a bemused tone, "Oh, it is President Reed, isn't it?"

I shared this funny little story several times before I realized what a parable it is. If you have never felt "boxed in" by life, you are very fortunate. However, sooner or later life will close in on you. When it happens, we are schooled to push the right buttons. Physicians, therapists, and caregivers of various kinds are supposed to make us better. Often they do, but sometimes they are unable to open the doors. So we reach for the "telephone" of prayer, but the compartment is empty. Even earnest prayer produces no positive results. Time for the emergency bell. We turn it on, or at least we think we do. We go to church and back again, and the bell is ringing loudly in our ears, but no one seems to notice. We even play the old reliable tunes like "Victory in Jesus," but the door remains shut.

First-phase spiritual claustrophobia! About this time, the voice on the other side of the door asks, "WHO ARE YOU?" We respond as "officially" as we can, "I am a child of God! A beloved **CHILD OF GOD!**" Our raised voice exhibits second-phase spiritual claustrophobia.

"**OH, NO, YOU'RE NOT!**" says Satan, and we are almost inclined to believe him sometimes.

But Satan is a liar, and he is wrong. It is true that we must sometimes wait for the deliverance. Daniel prayed for an angel to deliver him, but the angel was delayed. Paul prayed three times to be delivered from his "thorn in the flesh" and was finally told that he must endure affliction to learn the lessons of "strength in weakness" (II Cor. 2:7-10). But in due time (it may be at the last day) every voice will confess—even the voice of Satan—that Jesus is Lord to the glory of God the Father. The delay in deliverance is just a "circuit breaker." Even Satan must confess, "Oh, this really is a child of God, after all."

A phrase from Colossians is again appropriate: "You are not to be disqualified by the decision of people who go in for self-mortification and angel-worship"(2:18). I have heard well-intentioned persons "disqualify" some believer as a child of God because the healing had not yet arrived. Such disqualification has distressed me greatly. It is "spiritual abuse." It is the strategy of Satan to bring a "spiritual defeat" from a physical ailment.

In this life, we will experience some "box" of physical distress. The "box" may last for a brief time, as mine did, or it may endure for a long time, as it has in Barbara's case. In the last day, the "door will open," and we will all stand in the presence of the King, perfect in the spirit and with perfect, resurrected bodies. Glorification alone is the ultimate healing. In heaven, all of the redeemed will celebrate our healing.

* ◦ ●◗○◖● ◦ *

Discoveries on the Way

I do not understand unanswered prayers. I can understand in some generic way that God is sovereign and must carry out His will in His way so that He cannot be taking orders from the millions on earth who would direct Him.

But when it comes to specifics, I have a hard time understanding. I don't know why He healed me and does not heal another. I cannot know what tragedy I might encounter tomorrow that would make this healing seem meaningless.

But I do believe in the sovereignty of God, and I do believe in His goodness. And I believe in these attributes not merely in some generic sense, but I believe in them for every person in every situation.

Epilogue

As I indicate in these pages, I have no claim to special insights into healing. Nor do I claim any special "gift." But there is a brief epilogue to "my" story that demonstrates that "God's stories" are always open-ended.

In September following my healing I was to preach at the Atlanta First Church of the Nazarene on a Sunday morning. Some suggested that I tell my healing story. It seemed the right thing to do.

The people were especially responsive. They seemed to relive the story with me. At the very end of the service I yielded to an impression that I should invite those who wished to be anointed for a physical ailment to come forward. I thought that there might be two or three from this large audience. To my surprise some thirty or forty people came forward to kneel at the altar.

As the elders and I moved among them, anointing and laying on hands, I noticed that one woman was assisted to a seat on the front pew. As it came time for me to move in her direction, my heart sank. I saw the unmistakable bronze color of skin that identifies a liver patient, and as I arrived at her side she lifted eyes that showed the yellow hue. She explained that she had suffered hepatitis C for a number of years, that she was suffering extreme cirrhosis of the liver, and that the doctors had indicated that there was nothing more they could do for her.

I felt apologetic for raising her expectations. I felt like saying, but did not, "I have no power for healing. I am sorry to raise your hope by my testimony." What I did say was "My dear sister, the Scripture calls us to anoint and pray for the sick, and that is what we are going to do. We will trust the God who is sovereign and who is good." There was a sweet and fervent spirit as we prayed.

In about a month I received a letter from the woman we anointed. She identified herself as Mae Ewing and enclosed reports from the doctors indicating that her liver was unexpectedly regenerating. That news blessed me.

But a letter, even one that contains the doctor's records, cannot equal a personal encounter. A little over a year later I was speaking at the Senior Adult Retreat at Camp Adrian in southern Georgia. As I moved into the cafeteria, a woman with a radiant smile met me. She said, "You may not remember me but I am the woman whom you anointed a year ago in September, the one who was in the advanced stages of hepatitis C." I could not believe my eyes. Her skin was fair. Her eyes were clear. She showed no sign of the illness that had so devastated her earlier. We rejoiced together.

I am convinced that God, in His providence and goodness, provides healing from time to time in order that His name might be glorified. I am also persuaded that in His wisdom He sometimes provides the only ultimate healing by way of the glorification of the body at the time of death.

If you should have a story of healing I would be happy to hear from you. Write to me at the address below.

The story of healing will go on and on until He comes again.

Millard Reed

Trevecca Nazarene University
333 Murfreesboro Road
Nashville, TN 37210